Nonconfrontation Selling…
The One-on-One Revolution

Nonconfrontation Selling… The One-on-One Revolution

John R. Downes

Writers Club Press
San Jose New York Lincoln Shanghai

Nonconfrontation Selling...The One-on-One Revolution

Writers Club Press
an imprint of iUniverse.com, Inc.

For information address:
iUniverse.com, Inc.
620 North 48th Street, Suite 201
Lincoln, NE 68504-3467
www.iuniverse.com

ISBN: 0-595-00750-3

Printed in the United States of America

*For the hundreds of automobile dealers and thousands of sales-people and seminar students who discovered NonConfrontation Selling (NCS) and joined **The One-on-One Revolution**. Special thanks to Denny Waltermire, Larry Leonardo, Ken Nelson, Bill Smith, Joyce Signer, Ed Jezowsky, Jule Herford, Brooks and John Biddle, Harvey Harper, Renard Bergstrom, Henry Schmitt, Steve Grindstaff, Jennifer Zurlini, Ric Messinger, Doug Chell, Geoffrey and Scott Downes, Roy Crosswhite, Tom Coward, Bob Stephens, Jim Lamparter, Graye Wolfe, Bill and Jamie Pierre, Vic Pestrin, Harry Stein, Ruben Baca, Frank McClure, Bob (the Old Dutchman) Vandegrift, and Rainer Josenhanss.*

It is your human environment that makes climate.

—MARK TWAIN

It is a profound mistake to think that everything
has been discovered; as well think the horizon
the boundary of the world.

—ANTOINE LEMIERRE

Contents

Foreword

As CEO of the largest VW Porsche Audi distributor in the United States and prior to that sales manager of imported Ford products for Ford International Division, I had a great overview of the wholesale car business. But, after I entered the retail car business in 1981 and became a six franchise megadealer in Florida, I discovered John Downes' NonConfrontation Selling NCS program. Its fundamental differences from the existing status quo literally took my breath away. It's the opposite of the public's perception of salespeople and selling practices. I'm deeply flattered about being asked to write the Foreword for his book, as I'm aware that a large number of major players (a literal Who's Who) have utilized his program over the years.

John's low-key manner belies his insight and great intelligence about the automobile industry and the selling game. Keep in mind…the public's perception during the entire twentieth century has been that of loud talk, loud jackets, unkept promises, misleading information, closing areas wired for sound, and no respect for after sales service; and my experiences with a multitude of sales trainers was like a camping trip to the city park. John's relationship was a trip to Venus…then beyond.

One secret of NCS, as John invented it, is that it is credible, honest, completely unexpected, and the only selling philosophy that truly puts the prospect at ease and ends the adversarial relationship between buyer and seller from the very outset. I began uncovering its nuances when all of my store managers and I trekked to California to see first-hand one of his guinea pig dealerships utilizing his entire philosophy. We spent a week there. After the third night I fired two of my managers and sent them home, as they'd resisted the basic premises, and opted to cling to the status quo. I became committed, though, because this new way to treat a prospect and simultaneously gain more profitability was my opportunity to professionalize the selling business. One month later, John came to Florida and personally taught his own program in our six dealerships.

John Downes' philosophy is a head trip and requires a completely open mind. Our sales volume increased. As did our gross profit. More important, our customers left smiling. All business-owners know the importance of that smile. Treat him right and in a few short years he'll be back to buy again…and again, because he trusts you. That solid relationship allows the making of profit without the hassle. I've used John's NCS program the entire time I owned my dealerships (14 years), and it never became stale. It's intrinsic to my PMA Worldwide Automotive Consulting firm, which allows me to expand its precepts around the world. My favorites in this philosophy have always been *Bambi Meets Godzilla, FBI Interrogation School Questions, and Genius Used Car Manager.* I've warned you that this is a head trip!

The most important thing for you to remember, dear reader, is that you should bless John for writing this book and giving you a chance to raise your sales, customer satisfaction, and income to a whole new level, regardless of whether you do it as an individual or as a business leader. His book will make *you* smile and make *you* money. If ever there was a time for his philosophy, it is now with the emphasis on customer satisfaction and after sales service as monitored by the manufacturers and experienced by prospective customers. You will have a happier work environment filled with high self-esteem and growing success.

Rainer W. Josenhanss
President, P.M.A. Worldwide
Longboat Key, Florida

Chapter 1

A Psychological Thriller

NonConfrontation Selling is the opposite of what the prospect anticipates, and precisely what he desires.

The very nature of selling implies a confrontation between the seller and prospect, since the objectives of each are at cross purposes to maintain a bargaining position and achieve economic gain. The seller wants full price...the prospect wants a big discount; the seller believes the trade-in is worth little...the prospects demands a lot; the seller wants a big down payment...the prospect prefers paying as little as possible; the seller wants a high payment...the prospect a low one. It's easy to wonder how a sale is ever made with so many opposites in the recipe; but after the value exceeds the cost, and the seller creates the illusion of a good deal, the prospect lets down his defenses, opens up his mind, discovers the appeal of the product or service, and allows a selling situation to occur. Ofttimes, however, salespeople repel prospects by expecting them to be 'buyers' within moments after they meet, aggressively pushing inappropriate facts and benefits at them before a qualification, and not obtaining the prospect's story. The retreating prospect isn't discovering any merits or matching up, but is instead striving to flee from the aggressor. Some salespeople confront the prospect at the outset with, "See anything you like?" or, "Can I help you?" If the prospect's response is, "I'm just looking," isn't that rejection? He might as well say, "Leave me alone," or "Drop dead." Most are too polite for that. If a first-time visitor to a church were greeted at the door with, "Are you going to join today?", would he choose to stay?

For over thirty years the author has worked with hundreds of automobile dealers and managers throughout the United States, Canada, and Australia who opted for NCS when they realized that a majority of their sales staffs were not getting prospect's names **and** showing the most expensive model first **and** allowing demonstration drives without accompaniment **and** arguing with each other about who should meet a shabbily-dressed prospect or one driving a clunker **and** offering thousands of dollars off the sticker price on the lot **and** saying derogatory things about prospect's present vehicles and competing dealerships **and** referring to uncooperative prospects as 'flakes' **and** claiming to have a committed customer, when in fact it was the salesperson's own commitment instead in the form of a 'would-you-take'.

The prospect never likes the first price. Or the first payment. Or the first trade-in allowance. Or the first interest rate. Or the first anything! Consider an example of a $20,000 vehicle that's marked down during a sales promotion to $18,000. The advertised price is simply the one the prospect won't like first. When the salesperson informs him of the advertised price, his banal reply is, "You've got to do a lot better than that if you want to earn my business."

"What price do you have in mind?" asks the salesperson, as though he expected the prospect to tell him.

"I don't know," replies the prospect, "but it sure as heck isn't going to be any $18,000, that's for sure."

And the confrontation ensues.

"I can't take this to the manager," says the salesperson, "until he knows you want to buy the car with some kind of an offer. Would you pay, $17,900?"

As the prospect continues to resist, the salesperson offers increased discounts. In other words, the prospect gets rewarded for not cooperating. "How about $17,800? $17,500? What do you have in mind?" The 'would-you-take' technique has been around since two days before water. How can anyone not realize that the salesperson is making the offer...not the prospect? And when the salesperson's offer finally gets so low that it's embarrassing for the prospect not to accept it, the salesperson takes his own 'offer' to the sales manager, who promptly rejects it. Subsequently, when the salesperson returns with the 'bad news', the prospect thinks he's such a poor salesperson, who can't even sell his own offer to his own boss. The prospect fires him. Most dealerships wouldn't mind so much, except that when the prospect fires the salesperson, he also fires the entire dealership, walks out, and purchases his newer vehicle somewhere else. Many salespeople have been taught to sell that way, then they become managers and teach their people to do the same. The process is generational.

Ancient Greeks invented the principles of negotiations. A basic tenet is, "Never represent yourself." It applies to the seller and the buyer. The craftiest prospect never represents himself. He understands negotiations. He claims to be there for a friend, or sibling, or roommate, or parent, or offspring, or Uncle Miltie, or co-worker...but never for himself. If prospects are good at negotiations, shouldn't sellers be even better? Many aren't. Some break this important tenet of negotiation at the outset. They ask questions like, "What do I have to do to sell you a car today?" "Can I show you what I have in stock?" Like lightning striking, the salesperson has made himself the target for confrontation. Is he the person who sets the prices? Or orders the merchandise? Or runs the store? Of course not. But, his language implies that he does. His ego limits his success. Even a prospect with zero negotiation skills gets thousands knocked off the price simply for mentioning that the price is too high. Ironically, prospects with good negotiation skills generally hold in high regard salespeople with good negotiation skills, but have no respect for salespeople without any.

Think about a businessman who intends to borrow money from the bank for his new building project. Does the banker inform him that he can say yes or no at the first meeting? Of course not. He's too cagey. He won't act like the Chairman-of-the-Board. It's non-productive. Instead, he'll say, "We're having our bimonthly executive loan committee meeting two weeks from next Tuesday to go over everything. Do you have any more information that will help?" The bank's system **gets** information from the applicant, but gives **none** until fully armed. When does the applicant meet the chairman-of-the-board, if ever? During ground-breaking ceremonies! The bank's decision-maker appears after the decision is made, not during negotiations. "Never represent yourself" is cardinal. Unfortunately, retail stores are filled with salespeople who act like the chairman-of-the-board. Their speeches are full of first-person pronouns. Examples include, "If **I** can get your payments down to…, if **I** can get you more money for your trade…, let me show you what **I** have in **my** inventory."

"Oh" thinks the prospect. "So you're the cause of my pain. You're the roadblock. You're responsible for all the figures. You're who I have to steamroller to get what I want."

The woebegone salesperson positions himself as the villain, and becomes the target for the prospect's confrontation over price, payment, down payment, and trade-in allowance. He succumbs by offering lower prices. When the prospect goes inside and discovers that the salesperson's alleged price reduction cannot occur, he gets angry. Wouldn't anyone call this practice deceit? Deceit is defined as promising something that one knows cannot occur. How does the reader like that technique practiced on himself? Why do many prospects visit dealerships with chips on their shoulders, expecting the worst, and evading the salesperson's approach? Because, they've had personal experiences with deceit being practiced on them, sometimes only minutes earlier at the dealerships they'd just exited.

With NonConfrontation Selling, the prospect must never meet or talk to the Chairman-of-the-Board before the result.

NonConfrontation Selling causes prospects to begin negotiating the amount of the down payment during a writeup procedure known as the Description. About ninety percent of retail vehicle prospects finance their vehicles. Lienholders appear on nine out of ten titles. Cash customers don't negotiate the down payment. When a prospect does so, he's become a payment buyer. When the reader discovers how easy that is, he'll wonder why the practice hasn't been done since the beginning of the automobile business…instead of concentrating on price almost exclusively.

NonConfrontation Selling speaks to prospects with such ingredients as FBI Interrogation School Questions, Comfort Zones, Commercials, asking questions about his answers, Star Quality, Matching Up, recognizing no-win questions and weasels, and avoiding direct and leading questions and lock language. Psychiatrists and psychologists aren't the only skilled questioners.

What about commitments? Isn't that what every selling situation strives for? Many potentially profitable sales are unprofitable due to a salesperson's low skill level attaining a commitment. Many make it too easy for the prospect, which in effect, drives him out of the store. Example: Suppose the salesperson has just presented a monthly payment. Regardless of the amount, many prospects will act shocked and dismayed…then counter with one significantly less. A common, improper response by the salesperson is eagerness and happiness, which, ironically, causes the prospect to wish that he'd responded with an even lesser figure. If his first counter was unreasonable, shouldn't the salesperson's response be woeful instead of gleeful? Joy implies reasonableness. Despair…the opposite. The inappropriate emotion by the salesperson doesn't make sense to the prospect, whose only recourse is to visit another dealership and solicit an even lower figure? The salesperson must build just-right tension. It's like taking the slack out a rubber band, while making use of Loose Language and employing a Stairstep Commitment. The Teeter Totter, a playground toy, represents one of the greatest principles of negotiations to enhance profit. It's utilized in every situation following a Commitment. There's even a Double Teeter Totter. And a Double-Double Teeter Totter. Other elements include Valuating the Trade, Broken Record, Real World, working the prospect on his figures, Planting the Seed, Weasels, Bambi meets Godzilla, Oscar Presentation, the Telephone, and more.

What's the most important rung (selling step) on a ladder? They're all equally important. One that's flawed will cause a misstep. This book divides each selling step and most procedures into chapters.

NonConfrontation Selling is a learned chain of tenets, skills, and presentations that augment and enhance negotiation ability, and promulgates a philosophy based on reason, common sense, and empathy. It's applied human behavior, a tremendous sales resource that gives the seller a huge sense of confidence, power, control over any situation, and flexibility,...a **psychological thriller.**

NonConfrontation Selling is the opposite of what the prospect anticipates, and precisely what he desires. Forward is the direction of the one-on-one revolution. Or is it a revelation?

Read on.

Chapter 2

Meeting the Prospect

When meeting a prospect, one must radiate an aura and excitement about the privilege and opportunity that will culminate in a lifelong friendship. The opposite is practiced by those seeking only instant customers and sources of income. Ponder why any salesperson would utter, "Can I help you?", when the hackneyed reply is, "I'm just looking."

Is rejection his goal?

Yet, a preponderance of salespeople invite resistance at the outset with such inanities as, "Are you buying or looking?" and "See anything you like?" and "Can I help you?"

The salesperson must be a friend first.

Some prospects with a mental chip on their shoulder are wary, aloof, and defensive from previous buying experiences; and they're prepared to dislike the seller. The first moments are crucial to a selling situation's success.

*   *   *

Some Roleplays

"Good morning," asks the salesperson. "Welcome to Walters Motors. My name is Andrew…Andrew Fairweather. What is your name?"

"Henry…Henry Hathaway," replies the prospect.

"It's a pleasure to meet you, Mr. Hathaway. Henry Hathaway. Is your name spelled H-A-T-H-A-W-A-Y?"

"Yes. That's correct."

True, the prospect can be resistant to this, but is not as likely. The text is polite, sociable, genial, and unexpected by many prospects. There's nothing to resist. The topic is the prospect's favorite…himself.

"Good guess on my part," says the salesperson. "Again, thank you for coming in today, Mr. Hathaway. My last name is Fairweather. It's spelled how it sounds. F-A-I-R-W-E-A-T-H-E-R. Andrew Fairweather."

Count the number of times the salesperson has mentioned the prospect's name. And his own.

∗   ∗   ∗

The following situation includes a man, woman, and child.

"Good morning," says the salesperson. "Welcome to Walters Motors. My name is Andrew…Andrew Fairweather. What is your name?"

"Henry…Henry Hathaway," replies the prospect.

"It's a pleasure to meet you, Mr. Hathaway. (to woman) What is your name?"

"Susan Hathaway," she replies.

"How do you do, Mrs. Hathaway," says the salesperson. "Susan and Henry Hathaway. Is your name spelled H-A-T-H-A-W-A-Y?"

"Yes, it is," answers Henry.

"Good guess on my part," says the salesperson. "My last name is Fairweather, and it's spelled like it sounds. F-A-I-R-W-E-A-T-H-E-R. Andrew Fairweather. (to little boy) What is your name, sir?"

"Josh," he says.

"It's a pleasure meeting you, Josh," replies the salesperson. "Did you folks have a long drive getting here today, or do you live close by?"

No individual was ignored. The salesperson proffered a warm, sincere greeting and his entire name, repeated his and their names more than three times, talked about their favorite subject...them, treated each equally, avoided statements they could resist, and strived to radiate excitement about the privilege and opportunity of meeting them that could culminate in a lifelong friendship.

Regardless of a salesperson's skill level, he'll meet unresponsive prospects occasionally and not match up. Let's face it, some people browbeat their grandmothers. Others are candidates for the wax museum with their uncommunicative demeanors. Some may have just departed another dealership with negative feelings.

*   *   *

More difficult situation:

"Good morning," says the salesperson. "Welcome to Walters Motors. My name is Andrew...Andrew Fairweather. What is your name?"

"That's not important," answers the man. "We're just looking. Can't stay long."

"Mr. Walters always considers it a personal compliment," replies the salesperson, "when people choose to visit our facility to look for a newer vehicle. He's arranged for a large selection of vehicles to be here today for you to look at. One of the best selections we've had. I'll be right over here in case you have a question about any particular one." He starts to move away. "By the way, you didn't happen to come in on our ad today, did you?"

"I don't know," replies the man. "What's in your ad?"

The salesperson keeps his distance. "Lots of different models," he says. "If you're looking for a family sedan, small pickup, SUV, sports car, van, station wagon or what...I can tell you straight out if it's in our ad".

"Well, we are looking for something small and economical," says the man.

"We have two vehicles in our ad that meet that description," states the salesperson. I feel lucky. Follow me." He strides ahead of them toward some vehicles. "I'll show you where they are, at least." He glances back at them. "By the way, I don't know if I told you my name. It's Andrew...Andrew Fairweather? What is your name?"

"Harvey...Harvey Milner," replies the man.

"Harvey Milner," repeats the salesperson. "It's a pleasure to meet you, Mr. Milner. Is that M-I-L-N-E-R?"

"Yes. That's right," answers the man.

The prospect was initially unresponsive and "Just looking." The salesperson backed off, gave them space, then asked, "You didn't happen to come in on our ad today, did you?

Even the most unresponsive, jaded prospect finds it difficult to ignore that question, because an ad implies lower cost, saving money, and bigger selection. That accompanied with the action of the salesperson backing off made the prospect more likely to respond positively. "I don't know, what's in your ad?" he'd asked.

What irritates prospects who wish to be left alone are salespeople who overwhelm, stand too close, treat them like buyers the moment they meet, and ignore their shunning body language.

*   *   *

Comfort Zones

Each prospect has a **Comfort Zone**...an area encircling him that he doesn't want another to penetrate. Encroachment causes discomfort. Comfort Zones vary in size. Some prospects experience discomfort when someone's within two feet...others can't tolerate ten feet. When the prospect stops and steps slightly backward as a salesperson approaches him, he's indicating to not enter his Comfort Zone. The salesperson must stop closing the distance immediately. The prospect will experience relief and less discomfort from the salesperson's presence. The salesperson must continue his greeting from that distance…even if it's twenty feet away. The prospect will stand in place. When the prospect steps nearer, the salesperson may step nearer, but only by an equal distance. If the prospect steps backward, the salesperson must do likewise by an equal distance. It's a dance at long range. Ignoring a comfort zone can literally push a prospect right off the lot or out of the store.

An example is one involving a prospect who steps out of his vehicle and speaks first as he spots the approaching salesperson.

"How much is that truck over there?" asks the prospect.

"Which one?" asks the salesperson.

"That blue and white pickup," replies the prospect.

"Let's go see," replies the salesperson as he strides ahead of the prospect toward the pickup. "It used to be so easy to memorize the prices of all the vehicles when this dealership was smaller; but now it's practically impossible to keep all that in my head. Huge inventory. So many different models. By the way, my name is Andrew…Andrew Fairweather. Welcome to Walters Motors. What is your name, sir?"

The salesperson stops and offers his hand. If the prospect responds, the salesperson will gain control of the situation, because the prospect will be doing what the salesperson wants…not vice-versa. The salesperson will strive to stand in place during the greeting and fact-finding. The greeting's goal is to get the prospect to volunteer information. Comfort occurs when that is accomplished. In the foregoing, the salesperson created the illusion that he'd answer the prospect's query. The prospect relaxed. The salesperson began his greeting.

*   *   *

Another situation: A prospect stands alone on the showroom floor. The salesperson doesn't know if he's already been greeted.

"Good afternoon," says the salesperson. "Thanks for coming in today. Did you come to see someone who already knows you're here?"

If the answers is no, then the salesperson must proceed as though he were meeting the prospect out on the lot. If yes, then:

"Yes," replies the prospect. "Fred Blume knows I'm here. He went out to the service department to check on something for me."

"Fred's very thorough," says the salesperson. "If he takes longer than you're expecting, let me know, and I'll find him for you."

"Thanks."

"You're welcome. By the way, my name is Andrew...Andrew Fairweather. What is your name?"

"George Bernard."

"Nice to meet you, Mr. Bernard. I'll be right over here if you want me to find Fred for you."

"Thanks."

The question was, "Did you come to see someone who already knows you're here?" Another salesperson may have already accomplished a good greeting, hence the text is not redundant. The salesperson has only one chance to make a good first impression. It becomes the foundation for all that follows.

Chapter 3

FBI Interrogation School Questions

No prospect will ever appear with a biography pinned to his jacket, but most salespeople wished they would, because many prospects are reluctant to impart personal information about themselves before they match up with the salesperson. This makes customer-sense, because the prospect does not expect to like the salesperson, but instead is dreading the experience. Thus, the prospect's plan is to get information and give none. Sounds like an impasse, doesn't it? Enter the need for **FBI Interrogation School Questions.**

Their purpose is to attain information such as the prospect's name, employment status, one or more incomes, other family members, schools attended, residence, own or rent, present vehicles, and more;…a huge challenge in the sales process.

Question. If prospect information is so important, why do so many salespeople not obtain it before selecting a product to present? The answers are several: They're afraid. They don't know how. No one has shown them. The prospect is unresponsive. The prospect controls the situation. Let's examine a typical no-information situation.

A well-dressed prospect walks toward a lineup of pickups on the dealership lot, and a salesperson approaches.

"I want to take a look at a pickup," says the prospect.

"This one's our best seller," responds the salesperson. "How do you like it?"

"How much is it?"

"Would you like to go inside and see what we can work out? I know we can save you a lot of money."

"How much?"

Incredibly, situations like this occur. Mr. No Name Salesperson prattling with Mr. No Name Prospect. Afterward, the salesperson learns the prospect is a dishwasher at the local fast-food drive-in, his wife attends school, they and their two toddlers live with her parents, and their present vehicle is fifteen years old. Will the reader agree that the chances for selling this prospect a brand-new truck is about zero? In the above dialogue, though, the salesperson has caused price-dickering on an unattainable vehicle. Even if they go inside to "work something out," both will discover they've been wasting their time, and the prospect will depart without buying anything.

Incidentally, this prospect will purchase a vehicle somewhere within the next few days, and he'll be seen driving around in his newly-acquired, five year old pickup. But Mr. No Name Salesperson won't benefit, nor will the dealership he works for. Reverse situations occur, too, involving prospects with great wealth who dress down for the occasion and wear their grubbies. Some salespeople assume they're poor and either won't greet them at all or will show them too old of a vehicle and offend them. Even someone who's just won the state lottery is smart enough to know not to inform the salesperson of his available cash and good fortune, because by acting poor, he believes he can negotiate the price down.

"How much available cash do you have?" asks the salesperson.

"Not very much," replies the lottery winner.

Obtaining good information about a prospect is not the result of asking direct questions, but instead is the result of properly formulated FBI Interrogation School Questions. Let's take a quick peek at an incorrect FBI interrogation and discover why direct questions are inadequate. The prime suspect for a bank robbery, kidnapping, and murder sat at a long table facing the Inspector and the Chief in the Federal Building downtown.

"Did you do it?" asked the Inspector.

"No, I'm innocent," answered the suspect.

"He didn't do it," said the Inspector to the Chief.

"How do you know that?" asked the Chief.

"He said he didn't," responded the Inspector.

"Well, go ahead and release him then," said the Chief.

Is asking direct questions how the FBI solves a case? Then believing the suspect's replies? Of course not. Direct questions are not the proper way to obtain information. Wary folks withhold. The goal is to cause the prospect to want to volunteer personal information about himself and his family which will evolve into a two-sided dialogue instead of a one-sided monologue. A typical response to an FBI Interrogation School Question is one that goes way beyond the scope of the question and contains unasked for, volunteered information. As dialogue occurs, the salesperson must keep the flow of information going by asking questions about the prospects answers.

*   *   *

The Seven Most Wanted

FBI Question #1

"Did you have a long drive getting here today, or do you live close by?"

Sounds innocuous, doesn't it? But it's potent. The first characteristic to observe is that it's literally impossible to answer with one syllable. The prospect must articulate a complete sentence containing a subject and a predicate. One of the goals is to cause the prospect to talk in complete sentences which leads to compound/complex sentences which lead to paragraphs, dialogue and conversation. A typical response is, "Oh, about twenty minutes. We live over by the foothills on the North side."

The second characteristic, in this example, is that the response includes two complete sentences. Third, the prospect volunteers information that is not requested. The FBI question asks only about 'long drive', and the response volunteers a general location..."by the foothills on the North Side." Fourth, the purpose of the question is not obvious. Discovering where he lives is the purpose, but that wasn't specifically asked. Fifth, the question deals with the 'known' instead of the 'unknown'. The prospect is being asked about his most recent experience before he arrived at the store...his drive there. It's true that he could have taken the bus, cab, or trolley, but that's not likely; hence, the first FBI question is about a subject that the prospect knows.

If the question instead had been, "What are you looking for today?" (since the prospect hadn't found it yet) it would have become easy for him to begin a pattern of rejection by responding with, "I don't know. I'm just looking."

The verbiage of a properly formulated FBI Interrogation School Question is critical, every word must be used, or it won't work. Let's read why.

"Did you have a long drive getting here today?"

"No."

Did the prospect reply with a complete sentence containing a subject and a predicate? No, because the salesperson omitted half of the FBI question. The reader can wonder if it's better to cause the prospect to talk in complete sentences and commence a dialogue or to cause him to shrug, grunt, and become monosyllabic?

The gorilla at the zoo can do that.

Which way is more likely to lead to a dialogue and flow of information? There are no shortcuts for FBI Interrogation School Questions. It's all or nothing. Read the question aloud. "Did you have a long drive getting here today, or do you live close by?" When the prospect responds, the salesperson continues the flow by asking a question about the answer.

"Did you have a long drive getting here today, or do you live close by?" asks the salesperson.

"Oh, about twenty minutes," replies the prospect. "We live over by the foothills on the North side."

"Gosh, there's been quite a bit of new development and new construction in that area during the past three or four years, hasn't there?"

"Quite a bit, actually. We live in Brentwood Estates, and we like it pretty well."

"Brentwood Estates. That's nice. Aren't there some really nice homes, condos, and even apartments over in that area?"

"Yes. Ours is a home near the creek."

"Were you one of the first to live in that area?"

"Yes. We've lived there for almost four years now."

"When you say 'we', does that mean there are others in your family?"

The 'flow' continues because the salesperson asks questions about the prospect's answers, although, he's asked only one FBI Interrogation School Question so far. The prospect volunteers more information than requested, and he's responding with complete sentences, some compound sentences; and the result is a dialogue.

It's easy for the prospect, because he's talking about subjects he's familiar with.

Alternately, if the salesperson asked, "What are you looking for?" the prospect would have to talk about a subject he's not familiar with, because he hasn't seen what he's looking for yet, and the chance for a dialogue becomes more difficult.

Consider the amount of information the salesperson has about the prospect. He knows where he lives, an upscale subdivision nearby, that he owns a home in Brentwood by the creek, that he's lived there with his family for almost four years. Isn't this data helpful to the salesperson to determine the prospect's standard-of-living, lifestyle, income bracket? If the salesperson didn't practice the discipline about asking questions about the answers, he may have learned only that the prospect lives in Brentwood Estates, but not that he owns. Some people reside with friends, parents, co-workers, or rent...any number of cogent possibilities.

The salesperson has proceeded from the general to the specific. The FBI Interrogation School Question opens a general subject, and the reward for asking questions about answers causes the information to proceed from the general to the specific.

Let's digress for a moment to illustrate an inferior method that obtains some information, but develops no rapport, dialogue, or volunteered information.

"Where do you live?" asks the salesperson.

"Brentwood" replies the prospect.

"Been there long?"

"Yes."

"Married?

"Yes."

Question. Does the salesperson seem interested in any of the prospect's replies? No. How can he seem interested when he changes the subject after every monosyllabic response. Another question. Are the prospect's replies conversational? Only if you enjoy talking to the elevator voice. Read how few words the salesperson uses in his questions. The prospect follows suit. He's more likely to answer with complete sentences after the salesperson asks questions in complete sentences. More detail.

"Did you have a long drive getting here today, or do you live close by?" asks the salesperson.

"It took us about a half hour or so," replies the prospect.

"A half hour or so? What's a half hour from here?"

"We live out by Willetsville on Route 26."

"Willetsville. Gosh, that's pretty nice out there. There's been some new construction and development out in that area, hasn't there, over the past three or four years?

"Not too much, thank goodness. We have a farm house out there."

"Well, when you drive back there from here, are you on this side of Willetsville or over on the other side?"

"Our place is just before you get to the city limits."

"If you drive back on Route 26, what's the major crossroad just before your farm?"

"Thompson Road. In fact, that's where we turn off."

The prospect is giving the salesperson a verbal road map to his house. Was that his plan before he arrived at the dealership? Of course not. Yet, the salesperson obtains this information without confrontation simply by asking questions about the prospect's answers, and in the process he exhibits strong interest in what he is hearing. Will this increase the odds that the prospect may become more interested in the salesperson. Of course. There's another ingredient, which is paramount in the following dialogue. Make a statement about the answer before asking a question about the answer.

The salesperson replies. "Thompson Road. Oh sure. I pass there every time I drive out that way. Let me ask you, when you said 'we', in reference to where you live, does that mean it's not just you in your family?"

"Sure. My wife, and we have two girls," says the prospect

"Two girls. I have two girls, replies the salesperson. "And three boys. The way we worked it out was boy-girl-boy-girl-boy. They're still talking about it at the doctor's office. How old is your oldest?"

"Eight. And the youngest is six."

"What's your oldest's name?"

"Jessica."

"She must be in what, the third grade now?"

"Yes. She attends Willetsville Elementary."

"What about your youngest? What's her name?"

"Elie. She's in the first grade."
"Nice ages. Great names.

*   *   *

FBI Question #2
"Is one of the reasons why you live in that area because it is close to where you work?"

Discovering his employment is this question's goal, but its purpose is not obvious, because it's linked to a subject that's already being discussed...where they live. The questioner uses the 'known' to discover the 'unknown'. The question follows so closely in the dialogue about where the prospect lives that it seems a natural continuation of that subject. Exact wording is vital. The word "one" is utterly important. Don't omit it. Why? The prospect is more likely to respond conversationally. Eliminate "one", and the wording becomes "Is **the** reason why..." and the meaning changes to either it's the most important reason or is the **only** reason. But including "one" connotes that it may be one of many reasons, thus the odds increase for a dialogue and decrease for a one syllable reply. Returning to the prospect from Willetsville, let's continue with the second FBI Interrogation School Question.

"Is one of the reasons why you folks live in that area because it is close to where you work?" asks the salesperson.

"It takes about forty five minutes," answers the prospect. "I'm the district manager for Banana Computers downtown in the Tower Building."

"Banana Computers? What a big company. When you say you're the district manager, does that mean you're in charge of the entire department?"

"Yes, the marketing division. I oversee ten branch offices in a three state area.""What a big responsibility. Does that mean you have to travel a lot in your job?"

"Sure does, but my overnights average about two per week."

"Sounds like you really like it."

"It's challenging."

"Have you been with them for quite some time?"

"Ten years now."

"I've always wondered about that. When you retire from a company like Banana Computers, do you get a gold-plated mouse?"

"That's pretty good. I'll have to tell that to my boss."

One reason why this dialogue produces so much information is because the salesperson asks questions about the prospect's answers, and the result is a showing of great interest. If the prospect suspects that the salesperson's interest is not genuine , he'll clam up and become non responsive. Same if the salesperson expresses no interest at all. Reread the foregoing dialogue.

Doesn't the salesperson appear vitally interested in the prospect and where he works? Isn't he indicating that the prospect's work is important and that he's impressed with the prospect's success? Will the information that was volunteered assist the salesperson to determine how expensive of a vehicle the prospect can afford?

The salesperson could simply have asked him where he works, but would the answer, "Banana Computers," have been adequate? The janitor works there. The top-producing salesperson works there. The night watchman works there. The part-time office clerk works there. Their incomes are disparate. But, by first asking the FBI question to introduce the general topic, then asking questions about the answers and going from the general to the specific, the salesperson develops a good dialogue and information flow that is vital to the forward movement of the sales process.

If a prospect indicates that he's retired, the question 'retired from what?' should pop in one's mind. Bums are retired. Three star admirals are retired. There's a vast difference in their retirement pay. It's easy to realize that general information is not good enough when qualifying a prospect, so moving from the general to the specific is highly appropriate.

*　　　　　*　　　　　*

FBI Question #3

(To spouse) "Do you work outside the home?"

Watch a woman get riled by asking her, "Do you work?" Fire and brimstone commences, or at least an icy coolness that results in no sale. Of course the woman works. If she's a homemaker, she works twenty-four hours per day. The three word question, "Do you work?", implies that the role of the homemaker is not work. Instead ask, "Do you work outside the home?", and the inference becomes "Do you have two jobs?" That becomes a compliment to her work ethic and the role of a homemaker. Learning whether your prospect's family has two incomes is this question's goal, and like the other FBI questions, its purpose is not obvious. Two incomes can qualify more easily for an expensive new or used vehicle easier than one. If the answer is 'yes', then ask questions about the answers to learn what the specific job is in order to determine her approximate income.

*   *   *

FBI Question #4

"Are you looking for a vehicle similar to the one you are presently driving?"

The first product question. There's much to examine here. The prospect is very familiar with his present vehicle and can talk knowledgeably about it, thus this question is an excellent example of 'talking about the known to discover the unknown'. Savvy shoppers have a mantra they use when they wish to be left alone in a retail establishment..."I'm just looking." Notice that 'looking' is the third word in the FBI question. The salesperson's usage of that word makes it difficult for the prospect to use afterward as a shun.

"Are you looking for a vehicle similar to the one you are presently driving?" asks the salesperson.

The prospect replies, "No, I'm just looking."

Ridiculous, isn't it? The prospect is required to slow down and create an original rejoinder. As a result, he answers the FBI question directly. Let's start it again.

"Are you looking for a vehicle similar to the one you are presently driving?" asks the salesperson.

"No, I'm looking for something a little bigger," replies the prospect.

"What kind of vehicle are you presently driving?"

"A Honda Civic."

"Wow. You have a Honda Civic? What year is it?"

"It's three years old."

"Is three years how long you've owned it?"

"Yes. I bought it new."

"Is your Civic a two-door or a four-door?"

"It's a two-door."

"So, when you say you're looking for something a little bigger, are you looking for something bigger in a two-door or a four-door?"

"I think a four-door this time."

"Is one of the reasons why you're looking for something bigger this time because of your family?"

"Yes. With our two kids getting bigger, the Civic is just too small for us."

"If you get another vehicle, who would drive it the most?"

"I would. My wife has her Oldsmobile to drive around in."

The prospect is actually informing the salesperson what he's looking for by describing his present vehicle and the changes he'd like. His description of the 'known' vehicle better enables the salesperson to select the 'unknown' replacement for it.

*　　　*　　　*

Another situation. Same FBI question. The prospect has three possible responses, 1) Bigger; 2) Smaller; 3) Same size.

"Are you looking for a vehicle similar to the one you are presently driving?" asks the salesperson.

"No," replies the prospect. "I'm looking for something quite a bit smaller."

"What kind of vehicle is your present one?"

"It's a Buick Park Avenue, four years old."

"Isn't your Park Avenue a four door?"

'Yes it is."

"Well, when you say you're looking for something quite a bit smaller, are you looking for something smaller in a four-door or in a two-door?"

"Another four-door would be nice."

A picture unfolds describing a vehicle that he's looking for, as the prospect comfortably describes his present vehicle, and the salesperson obtains this vital information before he selects a vehicle to show to this prospect.

*   *   *

FBI Question #5

"If you get another vehicle, will that make you a two-car family?"

Discovering whether the prospect is planning to trade in his present vehicle is this question's goal, and like the previous FBI Questions, its purpose is not obvious, but instead sounds like a compliment. "Are you rich?" "Will you have two cars?"

It's difficult for a prospect to be put off by a question that implies a compliment. A potential problem posed by asking the prospect directly if he's going to trade in his vehicle is that it implies that he's buying today, and wariness raises its ugly head. Even if it doesn't, the prospect can veer the conversation into "How much can I get for it?" Instead of steering into disaster, the salesperson continues the interview with FBI Question #5.

"If you get another vehicle, will that make you a two-car family?" asks the salesperson.

"I have an old truck at home that I use," replies the prospect, "but I plan to trade in my Buick if I find what I'm looking for."

In this case, the prospect uses the term 'trade-in' first.

*   *   *

FBI Question #6

"When you bought your present vehicle, did you pay cash for it?"

It's the only question that's eliciting a simple 'yes' or 'no', as its purpose is to determine whether the prospect is seeking to finance. Like the previous FBI question, it implies a compliment. "Are you rich?" "Wow, you can afford to pay cash for expensive things." The interview proceeds.

"When you bought your present vehicle, did you pay cash for it?" asks the salesperson.

"No, I financed it," answers the prospect.

*   *   *

FBI Question #7

"On your present vehicle, are there any features that you particularly like that you would like to have again if you replace it with another vehicle? For example, does your present vehicle have a stick shift or automatic?"

A payoff now occurs, as a complete picture of the desired vehicle is described by the prospect. Ironically, he's thinking only of his present vehicle. He's mentally inside his own vehicle. Again, it's the technique of using the known to discover the unknown.

"On your present vehicle," asks the salesperson, "are there any features that you particularly like that you would like to have again if you replace it with another vehicle? For example, does your present vehicle have a stick shift or automatic?"

"We both prefer an automatic," replies the prospect.

"How important is air-conditioning?"

"Very. It gets hot. We'd like to have power seats and power door locks, too.

"You know what? I think I have a couple of good ideas. Follow me."

The salesperson walks ahead of the prospect to the vehicle or vehicles he's opted to show, not vice versa; and he does it after he's obtained the necessary information from the prospect, not before. Everything the salesperson says has a purpose, nothing is idle chitchat. The FBI Interrogation School Questions have an order, and each response from the prospect forms a better picture in the salesperson's mind about the prospect, his family, occupation, lifestyle, and desired vehicle. If the salesperson learns that the prospect lives in a poor neighborhood, has a low income job, then proceeds to show him the top-of-the-line or a new model, of course the prospect will like the vehicle; but the challenge is to select and present not only a vehicle that the prospect will like, but one he can afford to buy. Show a mansion on Nob Hill and ask the client if he likes it. Of course. Who wouldn't? But, can he afford it? If not, can he buy it? No.

*   *   *

Microwave Store

The owner of a microwave oven store informed the writer that he'd been constantly unhappy about his salespeople showing prospects the wrong ovens. His advertising featured loss-leaders. When a respondent to his ads asked, "Is this the model in the ad?" and the salespeople responded, "Yes", and the prospect asked, "Does it do everything?" and the salespeople answered, "It sure does", and the prospect replied, "I think I'll buy it", she took it home and discovered that it didn't;—and customer satisfaction plummeted. The store owner requested a list of FBI Interrogation School Questions. Here they are:

1. Are you a gourmet cook?
2. How often during the year do you prepare a dinner as elaborate as one your family used to prepare for Thanksgiving?
3. How often do you entertain at home?
4. Are you so busy sometimes that you simply throw a tv dinner in the oven because you're so tired after work?
5. Are you looking for a microwave oven similar to the one you are presently using?

6. Are there any features on your present microwave oven that you really like that you'd like to have again if you replace it with a new oven?

They worked. His customers who purchased the cheaper ovens were the fast-food junkies, the high-line purchasers were those gourmets, who prepare elaborate meals frequently. But, one doesn't find out if one doesn't find out.

*   *   *

Singles Bars

Another acquaintance asked if FBI Interrogation School Questions could be utilized in a singles bar. Why not? The writer created a short list, advised the acquaintance to not change a single word, and asked for the results. Less than a week later the happy bachelor reported his findings. Here's a dialogue containing the list.

"Did you girls have a long drive getting here tonight," asked the bachelor, "or do you live close by?"

Felicity looked into his eyes. "About ten minutes," she answered. "We live together in the Broadway Apartments off of 10th."

"How convenient," commented the bachelor. "It's close to town and a pretty nice neighborhood."

"We like it," said Felicity. She smiled.

"Is one of the reasons why you two live there because it is close to where you work? (to Felicity) Let me ask you first."

"I don't," she said, "but Venus does. I work at the First National Bank in Highland Park, but Venus is attending beauty college on Broadway just three blocks from our apartment."

"Does that mean you can walk there, Venus? inquired the bachelor.

"Yes. Felicity always has the car," purred Venus.

"It sure is nice meeting you two," said the bachelor. "My name is Jason, Jason Argonaut. What is your name?"

"Venus Caldron. This is my roomie, Felicity Fox."

"Venus Caldron and Felicity Fox," repeated the bachelor. "Is it just the two of you there?"

"Yes. How about you?" asked Felicity.

"My roommate's meeting me here in fifteen minutes, replied the bachelor. "He works late."

What's his name?" asked Venus.

The reader can recognize the FBI Interrogation School Questions, and appreciate the discipline of asking questions about the answers, progressing from the general to the specific, and asking about the known to discover the unknown. In all endeavors they're useful, practical, and effective, not to mention fun.

*   *   *

Ironically, a dialogue containing **only** FBI Interrogation School Questions develops no specific information. Let's read why. The situation includes the salesperson meeting a man and woman, who are together.

"Did you have a long drive getting here today or do you live close by?" asks the salesperson.

"About a hour, I guess," answers the man. "I live over the county line in Brockton.

"Is one of the reasons why you live in that area because it is close to where you work?"

"Yes," answers the man.

The salesperson looks at the woman. "Do you work outside the home?"

"Yes," she says.

"Are you looking for a vehicle similar to the one you are presently driving?" asks the salesperson.

"No," replies the man.

"If you get another vehicle, will that make you a two car family?"

"No," replies the man.

"When you bought your present vehicle," asks the salesperson, "did you pay cash for it?"

"No," replies the man.

"On your present vehicle," asks the salesperson, "are there any features that you particularly like that you would like to have again if you you replace it with another vehicle? For example, does your present vehicle have a stick shift or automatic?"

"It's an automatic," replies the man.

"I've got a couple of ideas," says the salesperson. "Follow me."

What ideas could the salesperson possibly have? He obtained practically no information about the prospects, nor features for a desired vehicle. He doesn't even know if the prospect would prefer an automatic transmission on his next vehicle, only that his present one has one. He doesn't know if they're married. What's he going to show them? Maybe the tooth fairy knows. Properly, the salesperson must ask an FBI Interrogation School Question, get a response, then ask questions about the answers to develop specific information before he asks the next FBI Interrogation School Question. In the preceding dialogue, the salesperson didn't learn where in Brockton the prospect lives. Maybe he has a tent pitched on the creek. Maybe the salesperson assumed he's well-off because of his attire. Maybe he's a valet in a mansion. Maybe the salesperson watched him get out of an expensive vehicle. But what if the vehicle is borrowed or belongs to a friend or relative? The salesperson did not develop information regarding the prospect's employment, only that he works close to Brockton. And even though the spouse informed him that she does indeed work outside the home, where??...what?? And what features on their present vehicle would they like on a replacement vehicle if they get one? Zero information.

*   *   *

Memorize the seven FBI questions in the most logical order.

1. Did you have a long drive getting here today, or do you live close by?

2. Is one of the reasons why you live in that area because it is close to where you work?
3. (to spouse) Do you work outside the home?
4. Are you looking for a vehicle similar to the one you are presently driving?
5. If you get another vehicle, will that make you a two car family?
6. When you bought your present vehicle, did you pay cash for it?
7. On your present vehicle, are there any particular features that you particularly like that you would like to have again if you replace it with another vehicle? For example, does your present vehicle have a stick shift or automatic?

Now look at the list in total. Observe that the first three questions concern personal information. The last four are product-oriented. Personal information first...product information second.

On the reader's next shopping trip to any retail store observe whether the salesperson he meets talks first about personal or product information. If he asks, "See anything you like?" he flunks. Or "How can I help you today?" Or "The item you're looking at is one of our best sellers." Don't do that. Even the most untalented salesperson can show the wrong product for lack of information, which is bound to occur when he proceeds with inadequate information and false assumptions.

Reread the list of questions again. Is the word 'buy' in any? The word 'bought' is in the sixth question, but it's used in reference to their present vehicle. 'Buy' is a scary word early in the sales process, as prospects get defensive, and it must be absent from FBI Interrogation School Questions. Examples to shun: "Are you buying or looking?" asks the salesperson. "Just looking," responds the prospect. "Nice day to buy a new car, huh?" asks the salesperson. "I'm on my lunch hour," answers the prospect as he looks at his watch. "Can only stay a minute."

A final word on this subject...practice.

Chapter 4

Commercials & No-Win Questions

Why is it that prospects are sometimes better at asking difficult questions than salespeople are at answering them? Who are the amateurs? Who are the professionals?

Doesn't it make sense that an automobile salesperson, who supposedly sells a vehicle very day or so or at least several times per week and has dozens of contacts each month, should know how to easily handle difficult questions posed by amateur prospects, who on average purchase a new or used vehicle once every three or four years? Is the profession of selling vehicles a crap shoot or a practiced art? Let's look at **No-Win Questions** to illustrate. First, a definition.

A No-Win Question is one that no matter how it is answered, the answer is wrong. Four of the most commonly-asked No-Win Questions at automobile dealerships are:

1. What's your best price?
2. Can I get a vehicle like this one for $250.00 per month?
3. What's your current interest rate?

4. How much can I get for my present vehicle?

Suppose the salesperson directly answers the first question. The prospect's typical response is, "You've got to do much better than that!" Whatever price the salesperson mentions the prospect won't like. Hence, every answer is wrong. No-Win.

Suppose the salesperson says, "Yes", to the second question. Then, later in the sales process the prospect is informed the payment will be closer to $375 (because the term, down payment, and equity position in his present vehicle weren't part of the prospect's question or the salesperson's answer). Suppose the answer is "No". Confrontation results. The prospect departs. Who wins? Nobody.

Suppose the salesperson answers the third question. Will the prospect like it? Of course not. The prospect never likes the first figure, regardless of the amount. He can rebut a low rate with, "another dealership is offering zero percent financing."

So, what can a good salesperson say?

One of the the most difficult obstacles to overcome with No-Win Questions is to not appear evasive. No matter how hard some salespeople try, their answers are patently evasive. Others seek a commitment before responding. Example: "If the price is right, will you buy the vehicle today?" Or, "If we have a good interest rate, can we go inside and see if you qualify?"

The secret to dealing with No-Win Questions is contained in this paragraph. Practically all No-Win Questions are about a specific vehicle. Therefore, the correct response is a **Commercial** that ends with a question about the specific vehicle. Let's clarify.

"I saw a truck just like this one over at Acme Motors," says the prospect with a challenging sound in his voice, "and they said they'd sell it for $2000 less than you're asking? What will you do?"

"You're going to love my answer," replies the salesperson without hesitation. "I don't know how you happened to come to our dealership today to ask that question if you haven't done business with us before, but this company is one of the largest and fastest-growing automobile dealerships, not just here in this city, but in this entire region; and that's because it's owned and operated by the Walters Family. Our company has been under the same ownership for more than two decades now, and during that time we've done business with thousands of customers, many of whom have returned to purchase their second, third, fifth, even tenth vehicle from us. And nobody can be that successful and do so much repeat business with so many customers if we didn't know how to do what our customers want, need, and require. And, I'll prove it. But first let me ask you, are you looking for information about a truck like this one because this truck is similar to the one you are already driving?"

"No," replies the prospect. "I have a station wagon right now, but I've been looking around for a truck."

Observe who is giving whom information. At this point, the prospect is responding to the salesperson's question instead of vice versa. Why? Because the salesperson ended his Commercial with a question about the same subject that the prospect asked his question about...the truck. The prospect asked a question about "this truck", and the salesperson's answer ended with a question about "this truck." See how simple it is? Now all the salesperson has to do is to ask a question about the prospect's answer, and he'll further distance himself from the prospect's question.

"Oh," comments the salesperson. " you have a station wagon right now? What kind is it?"

And the prospect will continue answering the salesperson's questions, providing he keeps the initiative. An alternate ending to the foregoing Commercial is:

"And, I'll prove it," says the salesperson. "But, first let's see if this truck is one you like at least as much if not a whole lot better than the one you saw over at Acme. Are you looking for information about this particular truck because it's similar to the one you are presently driving?"

It's a tactical error to challenge the similarity between the two vehicles, because the conversation will become argumentative. The salesperson cannot disprove the prospect's claim.

        *   *   *

Another situation. Syntax variation.

"I was visiting my aunt in Denver last week," says the prospect, "and while I was there I went to a dealership and saw a car just like this one. Same equipment and everything. But, they were having a big sale and their price was $3000 less than this one. I happen to live around here, and I would prefer to do business locally, so if you can meet that price, that's what I'm interested in. Can you?"

"You're going to love my answer," responds the salesperson coolly. "I don't know how you happened to come here to our dealership to ask for information about a vehicle if you haven't done business with us before, because a lot of people don't know just how big, vast, large, and enormous our company is. It may not look like it, but this is one of the most stable. oldest dealerships, not only in this county, but in this whole part of the state. It has been under the same ownership and management for more than two decades, and during that period of time we've done business with thousands of customers through the years, many for their second, third, fifth, even tenth vehicle. And, I know for a fact that Mr. Blatz, the dealer, will do anything to deprive any other dealership of the opportunity to do business with any customer. And, I'll prove it! But first let me ask you, is the reason why you're looking for information about a truck like this one because this particular truck is similar to the one you are already driving?

Even though the wording for the Commercial varied, the discipline of ending the Commercial with a question about the same vehicle that the customer asked his question about is imperative. Again, it's: "But, first let me ask you, is the reason why you are looking for information about a truck like this one because this particular truck is similar to the one you are already driving?"

The salesperson doesn't appear to be evasive, because he's not changing the subject, which is still the truck that the prospect is asking about. That's what it seems. But, the subject is really becoming the prospect's present vehicle. As a result, the salesperson becomes in charge of the subject being discussed. It's so subtle, it is unnoticeable.

*   *   *

When a prospect's No-Win Question is harsher, the Commercial follows the same format.

"Just give me your best price and no baloney!" demands the prospect. "I don't have time for games!"

"You're going to love my answer, sir," replies the salesperson. "I don't know how you happened to come to our dealership to inquire for information about a vehicle like this one if you haven't done business with our company before, because a lot of people don't know just how big, large, vast, and enormous our company is; but our company is one of the largest, oldest, most stable dealerships in this area, in fact in this whole part of the country, and that's because it's owned and operated by the Walters Family; and they've owned it for almost ten years now. During that period of time, our company has done business with literally thousands and thousands of customers, many of whom have bought their second, third, fifth, even tenth vehicle from us. And nobody can be that successful and do so much repeat business with so many happy customers if we were not able to do what our customers want, need, and require. And, I'll prove it. But, first let me ask you, are you looking for information about this truck, because this truck is similar to the one you are already driving?"

"No." volunteers the prospect. "I have a 2-door right now, and I'm looking for something larger."

"You have a 2-door?" asks the salesperson. "What kind of 2-door is it?"

After the prospect responds to the salesperson's questions, the salesperson can ask, "Oh, by the way, please forgive me, I'm not certain I introduced myself properly. My name is Andrew...Andrew Fairweather. What is your name, sir?"

*   *   *

The Commercial that responds to the Interest Rate question is slightly different due to the question's content.

"What's your current interest rate?," asks the prospect with disguised menace.

"You're going to love my answer," answers the salesperson with an unflappable and upbeat tone. "A lot of people don't know just how big, large, vast, and enormous this dealership is, and that's because it's been owned and operated by the same family for more than twelve years now. And, during that period of time, our company has done business with thousands of customers, many of whom have purchased their second, third, fifth, even tenth vehicle from us. Well, one of the benefits that gives all of our customers, and I am very pleased to be able to tell you this, is that the Walters Family has actually made arrangements with practically all of the major and minor financial institutions, not just in this area, but in the entire region, so that on any given day we can pick and choose from a variety of institutions, and be very very competitive in the marketplace. And, I'll be very pleased to prove it. But, let me ask you something first. Is one of the reasons you're seeking information like that because you might apply it to a vehicle similar to the one you are already driving?

"Yes," replies the prospect. "I'm looking for a truck to replace the one I already have."

As soon as the prospect responds to the salesperson's question, the sales-person does not need to answer the prospect's question. The verbiage in the final question is slightly changed. The verb, 'apply', is used instead of 'looking'. One **applies** interest to the transaction. The question to ask the prospect immediately following the Commercial becomes, "Is one of the reasons you're seeking information like that because you might **apply** it to a vehicle similar to the one you are already driving?" And very subtlely, the subject has been changed **from** "the interest rate" **to** the "vehicle he is already driving".

           *   *   *

Alternate wording.

"You're going to love my answer." replies the salesperson. "Honest to gosh, sometimes you have to read the Wall Street Journal and the National Review to keep track of the daily yo-yo activities of the Federal Reserve and the banking system in regard to rates and everything, but one of the joys I have working with this dealership is, you see, this is one of the largest and most successful automobile dealerships, not just in this area, but in the entire region, and that's because it's had the same family owner-ship for more than three decades now. Well, what the Walters Family has done is they've gone out and made financial arrangements with practically all of the major and minor financial institutions in the region. So, that means that on any given day, we can pick and choose from a variety of sources to assure being the most competitive. Let me ask you, is one of the reasons you are seeking information like that because you might apply it to a vehicle similar to the one you are already driving?

It's very important that the salesperson's answer not contain certain words that are in the No-Win Question. That's because those certain words will remind the prospect of his question. If we are trying to find a way to get away from the prospect's No-Win Question, why would it make sense to remind the prospect of his question? It wouldn't. Thus, words to avoid in the answer to the 'Interest Rate Question' are 'rate' and 'interest'. The reader should notice in the foregoing Commercial that substitute words are 'sources' and 'information'. Here is the word-ing in part: "…choose from a variety of sources…" and "…is one of the reasons you are seeking information like that…" The whole procedure would fail if the wording were, "Is one of the reasons you are looking for the lowest interest rate because…?" By having the words 'interest rate' in the answer, that will remind the prospect of his question, which is the exact opposite of the salesperson's objective for using Commercials in the first place.

*   *   *

Another commonly-asked No-Win Question.

"Can I get a vehicle like this one for $250 per month?" asks the prospect.

"You're going to love my answer." replies the salesperson. "One of the joys I have from working at this dealership, and a lot of people don't know this, but this dealership is one of the largest and most successful dealerships in this area, in fact in a tri-county area; and that's because it's owned and operated by the Walters Family, which has been involved in the automobile business in three states for more than two decades now. And, during that period of time, they've done business with thousands and thousands of customers, many of whom have purchased their second, third, fifth, even tenth vehicle from them; and no company can be that successful and do so much repeat business with so many happy customers if it was not able to do what its customers want, need, and require. And, depending on what you have in mind, if the vehicle you select is in the $260-270-275-280 range, right in there, then yes, absolutely. But, are you looking for information like that because you might apply it to a vehicle similar to the one you are already driving?

*   *   *

Another commonly-asked No-Win Question early in the sales process.

"How much can I get for my present car?" asks the prospect.

"What year is your present vehicle, sir?" asks the salesperson.

"It's a three year old Buick Park Avenue."

"Gosh, I feel so lucky. You happened to come in when Mr. Goodman, our used vehicle manager is on duty, and I know he'll be pleased to learn that your present vehicle is for sale. I know that he's with another customer right now, and he'll be a few minutes before he can get to it. While we're waiting, let me ask you...if Mr. Goodman is successful in purchasing your present vehicle, are you thinking of replacing it with a similar vehicle?"

"No. I want to get a Van this time."

The tactic here is, "While we're **waiting** for the Used Car Manager to take a look at your car…" The prospect is given a reason why the manager can't look at his vehicle right this second. He's with another customer. That's a good reason. It buys time for the salesperson to match up with the prospect and discover what type of replacement vehicle he may be interested in. The prospect feels like he's getting his own way because his question has been acknowledged. The salesperson continues the sales process through the Meet & Greet, Qualify, and the selection of a vehicle.

*   *   *

Prospects are very good at thinking of No-Win Questions. They don't even practice. Salespeople need to be even better at answering them. Commercials are the tools to accomplish that. Most No-Win Questions asked by prospects will be about a specific vehicle. "What's your best price on that truck?" "What's the monthly payment going to be on this van?" See? Thus, when the prospect asks a No-Win Question, the salesperson answers with a Commercial that ends with an question about the specific vehicle. The question must be tailored to the specific No-Win Question so that the appropriate verb fits the answer. Periodic review of this chapter is highly recommended. Being good is in the details.

For the reader to get good at this technique and apply it to his own situation, he must write his own Commercials for the most commonly-asked No-Win Questions. The Commercial needs to address the historic specifics of the company that employs him. Here are some facts to include.

1. How long has the dealership been in business?
2. Who owns the dealership?
3. How far-spread is the customer base?
4. What year was the dealership founded?
5. Other locations, related businesses?

Good verbiage includes, "It has hundreds or thousands of customers, many of whom have purchased their second, third, fifth, even tenth vehicle over the past period of time, and no company can be that successful and have so many happy customers if it did not know how to do what its customers wanted, needed, and required."

A good question to ponder is how can a company prosper, grow, and increase its customer base year after year, if its present customers felt they were not getting what they wanted, were not extremely happy, and were not well-satisfied? A company only prospers and continues getting bigger if it knows how to keep a large percentage of its present customers and is successful in adding many new customers each year.

Any company, regardless of how long it's been in business or the size of its customer base, can have great Commercials written about it. Prospects are canny, smart, devious, ambivalent, sophisticated, wary, frugal, and demanding. They're looking for a very professional salesperson.

Prospects know they're doing a salesperson a great favor bestowing upon him the privilege of customerhood. Much of their hard-earned money is at stake. The purchase of a vehicle represents most prospects' major investment for the year. It cost several months of their total income. It's reasonable for the prospect to expect top performance and professionalism from the salesperson they choose to do business with. It's their honor to bestow. They'll choose the salesperson they like, respect, trust, and who knows what he or she is doing. Commercials are customer-savers. And customer-makers. The slightest appearance of evasion causes failure. During the sales process, one never knows when the prospect is going to ask a No-Win Question. They occur unexpectedly at the beginning, middle and end. One should expect to be asked several No-Win Questions during each successful transaction.

Chapter 5

Anycar

When the salesperson learns **Anycar,** he can present any vehicle to any prospect at any time…regardless of the year, make and model. Anycar is synonymous with Anytruck and Anyused. Anycar contains twenty standard-mandatory features, which the salesperson should memorize and include in his walkaround presentation. Every car and truck will include at least fifteen of the twenty, which are referred to as standard-mandatory features. because the prospect cannot request to omit them. All are intrinsic to the vehicle.

A rule-of-thumb: Present Anycar features during the Walkaround Presentation…and the options during the Demonstration Drive. Ironically, most of the Anycar features are not mentioned by many salespeople, yet they add tremendous value to the vehicle. The salesperson who presents the twenty Anycar features will be a standout, appear knowledgeable and professional, and instill confidence from his prospect.

*   *   *

Twenty Standard-Mandatory Features

1. Engine size
2. Range
3. McPherson Struts
4. Electronic Fuel Injection (EFI)
5. On-board computer
6. Clamps, hoses & conduits
7. Accessible service points
8. See-thru fluid containers
9. Rack & pinion steering
10. Halogen headlamps
11. Front wheel drive (FWD)
12. Aerodynamic design
13. Wrap-around tail-lights
14. 5 mph bumpers
15. Ease-of-opening trunk
16. Size of trunk
17. Space-saver spare tire
18. Scissors jack
19. Cross diagonal brakes
20. Front disc brakes

Observe that the first eleven features are located at the front of the vehicle, the remaining nine are at the sides and rear. Learning them in the text order will provide a road map for a seamless Presentation.

Imagine a salesperson being able to make a masterful and commanding presentation of a vehicle he's never seen, yet that's the purpose for memorizing the Anycar features. Imagine the prospect's admiration and delight when he compares the Anycar presentation to what he may have been subjected to at a competing dealership.

*   *   *

Talking Points

1.Engine size

Every vehicle has an **Engine Size.** The factory has stamped the engine size on the block, sometimes on the radiator cap, and always on the window sticker. Some manufacturers such as Daimler-Benz and BMW are so proud of their vehicle's engine sizes that they've named trim-levels after them, i.e. 300D or 325i. 3.5L in chrome letters on the side of a vehicle indicates that the engine size is 3.5 liters.

2.Range

How far the vehicle can go on one full tank of fuel is the **Range.** Range is superior to discussing mileage. The only exception is the vehicle with the highest mileage rating of all makes and models. The mileage question is a trap. Consider the following:

"What's the mileage?" asks the prospect.

"Mr. Johnson," responds the salesperson, "the gas mileage on this vehicle is thirty-four miles per gallon highway and twenty-three miles per gallon in the city."

"We were just looking at a Hyundai that gets fifty-five miles per gallon." Ouch!

Recommended dialogue:

"What's the mileage?" asks the prospect.

"Mr. Johnson," responds the salesperson, "you can fill up the tank, go on a trip two hundred twenty five miles away—then drive all the way back without once stopping for gas…"

Anycar has a Range of between four hundred twenty and four hundred seventy five miles on one tank of gas. Why cross swords with a prospect if it can be avoided? Mention Range instead of mileage. If the prospect has a lake cabin one hundred miles away, for example, the dialogue can be:

"Mr. Johnson," says the salesperson, "you can fill up the tank here in town, drive all the way up to your lake cabin, drive all the way back, return to your lake cabin, drive all the way back into town a second time, and still have enough gas to get back and forth to work for a few days before you'd have to return to the pump for a refill. It's an engineering marvel...etc..."

The salesperson then discusses another Anycar feature and continues his presentation of the vehicle. He doesn't simply stop talking, stare at the prospect, and wait for him to re-ask the mileage question. Some prospect's internal dialogue might be, "Wow, I didn't know that!" or "I always have to fill up at the lake!" or "My present vehicle can't do that!" The salesperson needs to express himself in a unique, wow-filled manner to separate himself from salespeople who don't.

3.McPherson Struts (or) Iso-Struts

Iso-Struts, part of the state-of-the-art suspension system on the vehicle, contain nitrogen gas, which do not allow air bubbles to form inside like the old-style shocks used to. That assures a nice easy ride and more comfort for the driver and passengers. Reduced wear-and-tear on the vehicle during extended bumpy road driving enables the vehicle to hold a higher value, which will pay off for the owner at trade-in time.

4.Electronic Fuel Injection (EFI) and

5.On-Board Computer

The **Electronic Fuel Injection** system works in partnership with the **On-Board Computer,** which monitors thousands of engine functions per second. For example, it regulates the gas flow and the air mixture, maximizing the engine performance along with fuel economy during every minute of every drive. One can travel from the high desert to the low valley without having to purchase a different grade of gasoline to compensate for the difference in altitude, temperature, elevation, and humidity. And, on the hottest and most wintry days, the engine will start right up, because the Electronic Fuel Injection directs and controls the operation of the engine for trouble-free driving...and a lot of peace-of-mind. It's much like having a mechanic right underneath the hood. And he doesn't need a room at Best Western.

6.Clamps, Hoses & Conduits

A few years ago, the automobile manufacturers laid all the hoses over the engine block, which became the prime reason why engines heated up. Now, in the engine compartment, there are dozens of small **clamps** and fittings holding the **hoses** and **conduits** away from the hot parts of the engine. They're molded and shaped to go around the corners and ends of the engine so as not to touch the hot block. It's a good example of how the manufacturer is really concerned about their customers having care-free and trouble-free driving.

7.Accessible Service Points

With the tendency toward self-serve gas stations these days, practically no one looks underneath the hood anymore during a gas fill up to check the oil and fluid levels. So, the manufacturer has made it particularly easy for the driver of the vehicle to do so himself by providing **Accessible Service Points**. The oil stick and brake fluid stick are located in easy-to-get-to locations, which allow the driver to check fluid levels while wearing white gloves.

8.See-Thru Fluid Containers

The customer no longer needs to take off the radiator cap on scorching days to check the coolant level—and have a geyser steam-clean his face, because the vehicle has **See-Thru Fluid Containers**...allowing the driver to see-at-a-glance the fluid level. The same is true for the windshield wiper fluid.

9.Rack & Pinion Steering

This important feature gives the driver control over the steering of the vehicle, as it eliminates the 'play in the wheel.' Think of two gears that are engaged. One gear is at the end of the steering column, the other's attached to the front axle. When the driver turns the steering wheel, the vehicle responds immediately. If the driver has had a vehicle without **Rack & Pinion Steering,** he'd know it, because there was so much play in the wheel, and the driver had to turn the steering wheel quite a bit before the vehicle began to turn. Not very safe.

10.Halogen Headlamps

State-of-the-art headlamps cast a broader beam, can be seen from farther away, allow the driver to see greater distance; if a rock flies up and cracks the lens cover, the **Halogen Headlamp** will remain on, whereas, the old sealed-beams used to go out when that occurred. With Halogen Headlamps, the driver only needs to replace part of the unit instead of the entire unit, which helps make it more economical to maintain. Many people like the appearance of the Halogen Headlamps, too, in relation to the front design of the vehicle.

11. Front Wheel Drive (FWD)

The engine is mounted sideways…a transverse-mounted engine, and as a result most of the weight of the engine is over the front axle, which gives more control of the vehicle to the driver. **Front Wheel Drive** pulls from the front instead pushing from the rear, resulting in safer driving on wet, icy, and slippery roads. If the vehicle goes into a slide on snow-covered roads, the Front Wheel Drive will pull the vehicle back into control instead of pushing it out of control. And, because the engine is mounted sideways (given the overall length of the vehicle), there's more room in the passenger compartment, and the hump going down the middle of the floor (the drive shaft) is eliminated.

12. Aerodynamic design

Besides looking good, it improves fuel economy. A majority of makes and models have an **Aerodynamic Design.**

13. Wrap-Around Tail-Lights

This design element enables other drivers to see your vehicle from the side at night as well as from the rear. And, it actually enhances the appearance of the side of the vehicle.

14. Five Mile-Per-Hour Bumpers

When the vehicle hits something going five miles-per-hour or less, it will receive no damage. And, damage is reduced from higher-speed collisions.

Government regulations require two and one half mile-per-hour bumpers, but the manufacturers of this vehicle exceeds that by one hundred percent, because safety is such a high priority with them. If the prospect's present vehicle does not already have **Five Mile-Per-Hour Bumpers,** and he gets one with five mile-per-hour bumpers, there's a good chance his insurance rates will go down, because insurance companies look very favorably on the reduced costs for repairs on vehicles having five mile-per-hour bumpers.

15. Ease-of-Opening Trunk

When the trunk lid goes up, it stays up, plus it takes no effort to open once the driver turns the trunk key to unlock it.

16. Size of Trunk

Who'd think that a vehicle that looks small on the outside would be so cavernous on the inside, especially the trunk. If the driver has ever vacationed at the Grand Canyon, his first impression of the trunk size will be his second such experience.

17. Space-Saver Spare Tire

It takes no room at all in the trunk, because the manufacturer was kind enough to create storage space for it below the trunk floor. It has the same diameter as a regular tire, but it's approximately half as thick, which reduces its weight considerably. The old-style spares used to weigh about sixty, seventy pounds. Some people couldn't lift them out of the trunk. It's easy to use, takes up no room, and improves fuel economy because of its lighter weight.

18. Scissors Jack

It's superior to the old-style bumper jacks, because it fits into designated slots on the underframe, and it raises the entire side of the vehicle—requiring very little strength. When the vehicle is raised two inches, the tire lifts off the ground two inches. The old-style bumper jacks had to raise the bumper almost a foot before the tire even began to leave the ground; and a vehicle could slip off the jack sometimes on a grade or incline rendering it quite unsafe.

19. Cross-Diagonal Brakes (or) Dual-Diagonal Brakes (or) Split Diagonal Brakes

Think of two brake lines crisscrossing underneath the vehicle like an x. One is connected to the front right and rear left wheel; the other is connected to the front left wheel and the rear right wheel. If one brake line becomes incapacitated for any reason, the other brake line will still be in place connecting a front and rear wheel on each side of the vehicle, so that when the vehicle is braked, it will stop in a straight line.

20. Front Disc Brakes

If someone holds a coin with his thumb and index finger by the edges, another person can easily remove the coin from his fingers. However, if someone holds the coin with his thumb covering the 'heads' side and his index finger covering the 'tails' side, it's more difficult. That's the simple principle of **Front Disc Brakes.** They brake from the side of the drum. Drum brakes brake from the edges. Disc Brakes offer more braking power and are more safe. The factory requires Front Disc Brakes on all of its passenger vehicles, except the limousine-size vehicles and larger vehicles. Those have Disc Brakes all around.

Chapter 6

The Presentation

The **Presentation** of a vehicle should be a persuasive and impressive experience for the prospect, as the salesperson presents features and benefits that the prospect has never known. His mind whispers, "I didn't know that," and "Wow, no one's ever told me that before."

However, the Presentation's major objective is not to present the vehicle, as all the manufacturers preach,...it's instead to prepare for the Demonstration Drive. Consider this question: If the salesperson has a high percentage of Demonstration Drives, will he sell more vehicles? Of course. There's a huge reward for the salesperson whose presentation prepares the prospect for the Demonstration Drive...and who knows instinctively that the purpose of each selling step is to prepare the prospect for the next selling step.

Just as prospects volunteer information to properly-asked FBI Interrogation School Questions, so do they respond to Command Phrases during properly-executed product presentations. Once started and maintained, Command Phrases create an irresistible force, and this power is the epitome of persuasion and selling.

This chapter deals with the irresistible force that occurs with proper use of dialogue, Anycar features, Command Phrases, and the Presentation's important role for preparing for the Demonstration drive. The salesperson must cause the prospect to react to him...not vice versa...throughout the entire sales process.

Selling situations involve different numbers of people. Diverse scenarios include a single person, parents with two small children, roommates, father-daughter, prospect with maven, and so on. The first situation will include a husband-wife-child.

When the salesperson meets them, he must visualize where each will be seated in the vehicle during the presentation to prepare for the Demonstration Drive. Determining who the principal driver will be is imperative, because that person is usually the Decision-Maker. Exceptions are few. The Decision-Maker can be a homemaker, who does not work outside the home, if she's to be the principal driver of the intended vehicle. Even if the payment derives from her working spouse, the homemaker is considered to be the Decision-Maker if she's the Principal Driver. Principal Driver = Decision-Maker.

*   *   *

Eight Easy Steps

1. Overview statement
2. Present the engine and front of vehicle.
3. NDM experiences driver's seat comfort.
4. Present the left side of vehicle.
5. Present the trunk.
6. Seat child and NDM through right rear door.
7. Seat DM in front passenger seat.
8. Salesperson sits in driver's seat.

*   *   *

When the salesperson selects a vehicle, he must always drive it out of the lineup. If the ignition key is inside the building, he says, "I'll just pull it out so that we can take a better look at it. Oh! Let me run and get the key. Wait right here." He hastens inside, returns waving the key in one hand and holding the dealer plate in the other, walks to the rear of the intended vehicle and sets the magnetized plate in place, then starts the engine, drives it out of the lineup, and exits the vehicle to begin the Presentation. The vehicle is now showcased, a procedure symbolic of raising the curtain at a stage play. It's performance time.

In the following situation, the husband is the principal driver, thus the Decision-Maker (DM). The wife will be designated the Non-Decision-Maker (NDM).

Salesperson:

"Well, Henry and Susan and Josh, this is the all new Essex GLX, one of the leading vehicles in its class in the world today...a well-engineered masterpiece of automotive technology that's aerodynamic outside and spacious inside. It provides great safety and economy, with a ride, comfort, and convenience that I think all the other factories are green with envy about. Let me show you."

This is the **Overview** statement, much like the lead paragraph in a news story. It includes five of the six Broad Area Raygun Bullets, which are safety, economy, ride, value, ego satisfaction, and comfort/convenience. It can be used to present Anycar. Reread it several times thinking first about a Rolls-Royce, then a Volkswagen, Chevrolet, Toyota truck, Lincoln, Pontiac, et al. If instead, the salesperson said, "Isn't she a beauty?" and the prospect asked, "What can you tell me about it?" and the salesperson responded, "What would you like to know?"...would the prospect wish to reward the salesperson with his business? Why not insist on credibility, professionalism, and good performance?

The salesperson peers inside the open driver's door.

Salesperson:

"Susan, come over here. (Command Phrase) I want to show you how easy it is to release the hood. Reach down there and pull that lever." (Command Phrase)

She does.

Salesperson:

"See how easy it is? And it's inside the car for your security. Now let's go to the front of the car." (Command Phrase)

The family follows him.

Salesperson:

"I'll show you how easy it is to raise the hood. Susan. See that black lever? Simply take your index finger and pull up on it." (Command Phrase) "Feel it? Raise the hood. (Command Phrase) Feel its light weight?"

Susan:

"That's easy."

Salesperson:

"I know. Now Josh, take this bar and insert it in that slot there in the hood. (Command Phrase) Good. Thank you for helping. Just look at that engine. (Command Phrase) Looks like the reincarnation of Grand Coulee Dam, don't you think? This vehicle is equipped with a 3.2 Liter Engine, which is strong, dependable, efficient, and maximizes performance. For example, Henry and Susan, and Josh, you can up the tank, go on a trip two hundred twenty five miles away...then drive all the way back without once stopping for gas. An engineering marvel. But see that hump right there? And that hump right there? That's the encasement for iso-shocks, part of the state-of-the-art suspension system on the vehicle. They contain nitrogen gas, which does not allow air bubbles to form inside like the old-style shocks used to. That assures a nice easy ride and more comfort for everybody. Reduced wear-and-tear on the vehicle during extended bumpy road driving enables the vehicle to hold a higher value, which pays off at trade-in time. Iso-struts make you feel like you're riding in a limousine. So Josh, can you remember what kind of gas is inside the Iso-struts?"

Josh:

"Nitrogen?"

Salesperson:

"Good job. Another very important feature on this vehicle is the Electronic Fuel Injection (EFI) in partnership with the On-Board Computer. It monitors thousands of engine functions per second. For example, it regulates the gas flow and the air mixture, maximizing engine performance along with fuel economy during every minute of every drive. One can travel from the high desert to the low valley without having to purchase a different grade of gasoline to compensate for the difference in altitude, temperature, elevation, and humidity. And, on the hottest or most wintry days, the engine will start right up, because the Electronic Fuel Injection directs and controls the operation of the engine for trouble-free driving...and a lot of peace-of-mind. It's like having a mechanic underneath the hood. And you don't need to check him in the Best Western. Safety and peace-of-mind are high priorities for the manufacturer of this vehicle, and I hope you appreciate hearing that as much as I enjoy telling you."

Henry:

"Sounds good."

Salesperson:

"And, who'd think of this? But, see those Clamps right there? And there? And there? I've never actually counted them, but there are dozens of these Clamps in the engine compartment holding the Hoses and Conduit away from the hot parts of the engine. Years ago, the automobile companies laid all the hoses over the engine block, which became the prime reason why engines heat up in the first place. And look! These Hoses and Conduits are molded and shaped to go around the corners and ends of the engine so as not to touch the block or anything else! It's a good example of how the factory is really concerned about providing trouble-free driving.

And, the engine has very Accessible Service Points. Look at this, Josh. Right there is where you can check the oil level for dad at the gas station. I'll show you. Go ahead. Reach down there and raise up on that circle." (Command Phrase) "Right there. Now, take it all the way out." (Command Phrase) "Hold it out sideways." (Command Phrase) "See that line? That means the oil level is fine. But, if it ever gets down to that line right there, you need to tell dad to add a quart of oil. So, just put it back right there." (Command Phrase) "And here is where you add oil, Josh. Just unscrew and voila! Pretty fun and easy, isn't it?"

Josh:

"Uh huh."

Salesperson:

"Susan, look at these See-Through Fluid Containers. (Command Phrase) With the proliferation of self-serve gas stations these days, practically no one looks underneath the hood anymore during a gas fill up, so the factory has made it easy for the driver to do it. This one is the windshield wiper fluid. This one is the coolant in the radiator. You don't need to remove the radiator cap on a hot day to see if the coolant level is adequate...you can see at a glance. By the way, this vehicle is also equipped with what the factory refers to as Rack & Pinion Steering. It's the state-of-the-art steering system. This important feature gives the driver greater control as it eliminates the play in the wheel. Think of two gears that are engaged. One gear is at the end of the steering column, the other's attached to the front axle. When the driver turns the steering, the vehicle responds immediately. If you've had a vehicle without Rack & Pinion Steering, you'd know it, because there was so much play in the wheel, and you needed to turn the wheel quite a bit before the vehicle began to turn. Not very safe."

Up to this point the salesperson has mentioned nine of the twenty Anycar features: Engine Size, Range, Iso-Struts, Electronic Fuel Injection (EFI), On-Board Computer, Clamps Hoses & Conduits, Accessible Service Points, See-Thru Fluid Containers, and Rack & Pinion Steering. He's presented them in that precise order. Notice that the salesperson did not simply mention a feature. He mentioned two or three or more benefits provided by each feature. A feature without a benefit is worthless. And a feature with three or four benefits is far superior to one with only a couple.

Salesperson:

"Step back and look at those headlamps. (Command Phrase) They're the famous Halogen headlamps. State-of-the-art again. They cast a broader beam, can be seen from farther away, allow the driver to see greater distance at night; if a rock flies up and cracks the lens cover, the Halogen headlamp will remain on, whereas, the old sealed-beams used to go out when that occurred. With Halogen headlamps, the driver only needs to replace part of the unit instead of the entire unit, which helps make it more economical to maintain. Many people like their appearance in relation to the front design of the vehicle, what's your thought on that, Susan?"

Susan:

"It looks nice."

Salesperson:

"By the way, Josh, look at the engine? It's actually in there sideways. That's because of the Front Wheel Drive. The factory refers to that as a transverse-mounted engine. That causes most of the engine weight to be over the front axle, which gives more control to the driver. Front Wheel Drive pulls from the front instead of pushing from the rear, resulting in safer driving on wet, icy, and slippery roads. If the vehicle goes into a slide on snow-covered roads, the Front Wheel Drive will pull the vehicle back into control instead of pushing it out of control. And because the engine is mounted sideways…given the overall length of the vehicle…there's more room in the passenger compartment. And the hump going down the middle of the floor is eliminated. Henry, let me show you." (Command Phrase)

The salesperson walks from the front of the vehicle to the driver's door and opens it. Front Wheel Drive should be the last feature that the salesperson mentions during the engine presentation, because it serves as a smooth transition to Step #2 of the **Eight Easy Steps.** It's a logical continuation to be discussing how much more room there is in the passenger compartment because the "hump" has been eliminated and then showing it to them. No appearance of subject change.

When making a Presentation to three or more people, there's always one who's standing farthest away. The salesperson must refer to that person by name when moving from one part of the vehicle to another during the Presentation. Hearing his name and seeing movement practically requires him to move toward the activity; and ironically, he causes the entire group to follow.

Salesperson:

"Susan. Even though you've indicated that Henry does most of the driving, this is your big opportunity to see just how comfortable the driver's seat is. Get in." (Command Phrase)

Command Phrases

Susan sits in the driver's seat with no resistance. Here's why. **Command Phrases** are compelling. The salesperson did not ask Susan to sit down, he gently commanded her to. And he preceded the command with a reason. If he hadn't, the prospect may have opposed or ignored it or gotten defensive. For example, if the salesperson had said , "Susan, would you like to sit here in the driver's seat?" her defensive, yet polite rejection could have been, "No thanks. I don't drive much." But, the successful verbiage was difficult for Susan to oppose, as it acknowledged that "Henry does most of the driving..." which took that rejection weapon away from her; and it reasoned that "this is your big opportunity to see just how comfortable the driver's seat is." It culminated in the Command Phrase, "Get in."

Salesperson:

"Comfortable, isn't it?"

Susan:

"It's pretty nice."

Salesperson:

"Josh. Just look at how much legroom your mom has. Henry, can you see her legroom?"

Henry:

"Sure can."

Salesperson:

"Now Susan, Josh is going to adjust the seat for you. Josh. Give me your hand. (Command Phrase) See that red button next to the front seat? Push the back of it down." (Command Phrase)

He does.

Josh:

"Like this?"

Salesperson:

"Yes. Keep pushing on it. Good job. Susan? Feel the seat moving back?"

Susan:

"Yes."

Salesperson:

"Even more legroom. Here Henry. Let's get you in on this. Stoop down here." (Command Phrase) " See this lever? Press it back." (Command Phrase) "Susan, press against the seat back. (Command Phrase) Ahhh. Nice, huh?"

Susan:

"I'll say."

Salesperson:

"Josh. Your mom has a recliner. Nice for roadside stops on your trips."

Susan:

"This is nice."

Salesperson:

"Here. Let me put the seat back into the upright position. There. Hop out, Susan. (Command Phrase) Let's go back here."

Susan exits the vehicle. All follow the salesperson to rear.

Salesperson:

"By the way, the maker of this vehicle began doing something several years ago that has caused them to get a lot of ongoing notoriety, publicity and a very strong leadership position in the automotive world. It's the work they do to continue improving their design and aerodynamics. Do you keep up with the publicity, Henry?"

Henry:

"Good stuff."

Salesperson:

"When this model was first introduced, the sales so far exceeded projections that the factory has acted almost like a proud new father. About the only thing they don't do is pass out cigars. Thank goodness! And who would think of this? See the Wrap-Around Tail Lights? They wrap around the side of the car. This design element enables other drivers to see you from the side at night as well as from the rear. And, I believe it actually enhances the appearance of the design from the side. What's your thought about that, Susan?"

Susan:

"Looks good."

Salesperson:

"And when you look at this rear bumper, this vehicle is equipped with what the factory refers to as Five Mile-Per-Hour Bumpers. Government regulations require 2 1/2 mile-per-hour bumpers, but the maker of this vehicle is so safety-conscious, it chose to exceed that standard by one hundred percent. On the front, too! Thus, if the vehicle strikes something going five miles-per-hour or less, it will incur no damage. And damage is reduced from higher speed collisions. If your present vehicle does not already have Five Mile-Per-Hour Bumpers, and you acquire one with Five

Mile-Per-Hour Bumpers, there's a good chance your insurance rates will go down, because insurers look very favorably on reduced repair costs. When you think about it, in today's society there's just not much opportunity anymore to reduce costs."

The salesperson hands the trunk key to Susan.

Salesperson:

"Here, Susan. Insert the round key in the lock. (Command Phrase) Turn it clockwise."

Susan opens the trunk.

Salesperson:

"See how easy it opens and stays up. Who'd think that this vehicle would have such a huge trunk.? Look at all that room, Josh. Have you ever visited the Grand Canyon?"

Josh:

"No, I haven't."

Salesperson:

"By the way, Susan, is anything missing?"

Susan:

"The spare tire?"

Salesperson:

"That's right. The way the factory builds these cars, they just don't get flats anymore. I'm only kidding! What they've actually done is equip this vehicle with a Space-Saver Spare Tire that fits below the trunk floor. It has the same diameter as a regular tire, but it's about half as thick, which reduces its weight considerably. The old-style spares used to weigh about sixty, seventy pounds. Some people couldn't lift them out of the trunk. It's easy to use, takes up no room, and improves fuel economy because of its light weight. When you think about it, a spare tire is only utilized about one percent of the time, and it rides around in the trunk ninety-nine percent of the time, so why should it take up valuable space in the trunk? If you get a flat, put on the temporary spare, drive fifty miles or so to the next gas station, repair and replace the permanent tire, and hide away the Space-Saver Spare."

Some prospects suspect that the factory provides a temporary spare to save money. It costs more, because the factory only buys one for every four regular tires and wheels. Reducing about thirty pounds improves fuel economy…the factory's primary motive.

Salesperson:

"Henry, see what's holding down the Space-Saver Spare? That's the Scissors Jack. It's superior to the old-style bumper jacks, because it fits into designated slots on the underframe, and it raises the entire side of the vehicle…requiring very little strength. When the vehicle rises two inches, the tire lifts off the pavement two inches. Bumper jacks elevated the bumper several inches before the tire even began to leave the ground; and a vehicle could slip off the jack, sometimes on a grade or incline, rendering it quite unsafe. By the way, let me say something about the brakes. This vehicle is equipped with what the factory refers to as Cross-Diagonal Brakes. Think of two brake lines crisscrossing underneath the vehicle like an x. One is connected to the right front and left rear wheel; the other is connected to the left front wheel and the right rear wheel. If one brake line becomes incapacitated for any reason, the other brake line will still be in place connecting a front and rear wheel on each side of the vehicle, so that when the vehicle is braked, it will stop in a straight line. But, what if the brake lines were only connecting the two right wheels and the two left wheels? Then the wheels on one side of the car would be the only ones to stop, and the vehicle could spin and end up in a horrible situation. The factory has made Cross-Diagonal Brakes mandatory equipment on this vehicle, because safety is such a high priority for them. I hope you appreciate hearing that as much as I enjoy telling you. Speaking about brakes, Josh, very carefully remove this quarter from my fingers." (Command Phrase)

If the salesperson holds a coin with his thumb and index finger at the edges, it's simple for another to remove the coin from his fingers. However, if the salesperson holds the coin with his thumb covering the 'heads' side and his index finger covering the 'tails' side, it's more difficult to remove it. That's the principle of Front-Disc Brakes, which grip from the side of the drum, whereas Drum brakes grip from the edge of the drum. Hence, there's substantially greater braking power from Front Disc Brakes.

Josh:

"You mean like this?"

He easily removes the coin from the salesperson's fingers.

Salesperson:

"Yes. See how easy that was? Let me have it back. We'll try it a different way."

Josh returns the coin to the salesperson, who holds it with his thumb on the face and his index finger on the tails side.

Salesperson:

"Harder that time, wasn't it, Josh?"

Josh:

"Yes."

Salesperson:

"You see, Susan, I just demonstrated the difference between drum brakes and disc brakes. Drum brakes grip from the edge of the drum…like this, and disc brakes grip from the sides, like this. Disc brakes provide much more stopping power, and again, the factory has opted to make Front Disc Brakes mandatory equipment."

The salesperson could have simply said that the vehicle has Front Disc Brakes, but the prospects may not have known or understood what they are or what they do or how they work, or any benefits. All the reader need do to prove it is ask a household member to explain front disc brakes aloud. If the salesperson doesn't explain features and benefits, who will? Don't forget, a feature without a benefit is worthless.

Salesperson:

"Well, Henry, Susan, Josh…come around here and let me show you this." (Command Phrase)

He moves to the right rear door and opens it.

Salesperson:

"Susan, if you get another vehicle, you probably won't be riding in the back, but you'll be taking Josh and his friends places, and you may have company visiting occasionally from out-of-town. I want you to see how much legroom they'll have. Josh, hop in there first and slide over. Make room for mom." (Command Phrase)

This Command Phrase is a very important one during the Presentation, because it precedes the prospect getting into the vehicle. If the prospect balks, the chances for a Demonstration Drive are reduced. The salesperson's wording placed the Command Phrase at the end instead of the beginning. If he'd said, "Susan, why don't you hop in the back seat and see how much legroom there is?" she could have opposed it with, "I never ride in the back. I can see how roomy it is from here." But, the salesperson preceded the Command Phrase with a reason after he acknowledged that she probably doesn't ride in the back, and Josh and Susan both got in as though lead by an irresistible force.

Salesperson:

"There you go. See how much legroom there is? Roomy, isn't it? Here. I'm going to adjust the front seat even more. See how I do this, Henry? Check that headroom, Susan. Who'd think it would be so cavernous on the inside? By the way, Henry, while Susan and Josh are in the back seat, I want you to see for yourself how much legroom there is in the front passenger seat. Sit right there."

Another Command Phrase that's preceded with a reason. By now, these prospects are so accustomed to Command Phrases, they automatically obey. If they'd resisted early in the Presentation, they probably would have continued to resist, and the sales process would have fallen apart like a house of cards.

Now, all are seated in the vehicle as per the diagram. They don't have a clue that the salesperson is preparing them for a Demonstration Drive. How can they? All the doors are open, the trunk and hood are raised. The salesperson didn't ask them to get in the vehicle so they could go on a test drive, only to see the legroom and feel the comfort of the seats. If during the Presentation, the salesperson had closed the hood before moving to the driver's door, it could have created the impression there was nothing further to know or say about the engine. Finis! The end! However, when the hood remains open, it conveys there is more to learn. Moreover, if he'd shut the rear door after Susan and Josh had "hopped in the back seat", mother and son would have been separated from dad, and they may have strived to exit the other side. But the salesperson controlled their movements with the door open while he seated the remaining family member. Everyone participated in the performance. Open doors, hood, and trunk are ostensible clues that no one's going anywhere. The seating of the salesperson in the driver's seat is the remaining challenge to assure a Demonstration Drive.

Salesperson:

(to Henry) "Nice isn't it? And notice how this seat is independent from the driver's seat, so that you sit back farther than the driver. By the way, Susan and Josh, lean forward. (Command Phrase) Look at the storage compartment in the front for maps and things for trips. There's an excellent sound system in this car. In fact, let me go around to the other side so I can show it to you. Oh, I'd better close the trunk first."

The salesperson hastens to the rear of the vehicle, shuts the trunk, returns to the front as he closes the right-side doors, then shuts the hood as he walks around the front of the vehicle to the driver's seat, sits down, and shuts the door.

Salesperson:

"I just love the comfort of these seats. I'd like to ask my boss to order one for me so that I can enjoy it in my living room. It's a good idea to turn on the engine before turning on the radio. Less drain on the battery. Oh, Susan, remember my mentioning the Electronic Fuel Injection? I want you and Josh to observe I won't step on the gas pedal when I start the engine. Lean forward so you can see. (Command Phrase) In fact, Henry, you start it. (Command Phrase) I'll do nothing. Turn the key." (Command Phrase)

   Henry starts the engine.

Salesperson:

"Started right up. By the way, Josh, what station do you listen to?"

Josh:

"KPUK. 93.9."

Salesperson:

"There. That's it, isn't it? Just like sitting in the front row of a Bruce Springsteen Concert, what do you think?"

Josh:

"Sounds good."

Salesperson:

"Here's the fader. Listen to those rear speakers. Now to the right side…now to the front. I like to refer to the sound system in this vehicle as concert hall sound. Let me turn it down. I want to show you how smoothly the car shifts from neutral into reverse. You do it, Henry. (Command Phrase) Move that lever from N to R. (Command Phrase) Now shift it from reverse to drive." (Command Phrase) There. Pretty smooth, huh?"

And off they go on the Demonstration Drive. The Decision-Maker started the car, put it into gear, and enabled the salesperson to commence the next selling step…the Demonstration Drive. The foregoing situation covered every step of the procedure and presented all twenty of the Anycar features.

*   *   *

Eight Easy Steps

1. Overview statement
2. Present the engine and front of vehicle.
3. NDM experiences driver's seat comfort.
4. Present the left side of vehicle.
5. Present the trunk.
6. Seat child and NDM through right rear door.
7. Seat DM in front passenger seat.
8. Salesperson sits in driver's seat.

Varied scenarios alter the steps. With a solo prospect, eliminate numbers three and six; an aggressive Non-Decision Maker can switch roles with the Decision Maker; a 2-seater will not provide room for three persons on a Demonstration Ride.

*   *   *

Practicing Perfection Makes Perfect

1.   Memorize the 20 Anycar Features in order.
2.   Present each Feature with two or more benefits.
3.   Memorize the 8 Steps of the Presentation.
4.   Be good at Command Phrases.
5.   Precede Command Phrases with the reason when inviting inside.
6.   Refer to the person farthest away by name.
7.   Ask prospects about Features and Benefits, not how they like the vehicle.
8.   Involve each group member in the performance.
9.   Consider each group member equally important.
10. Present Standard-Mandatory Features during the Presentation... optional equipment during the Demonstration Drive.

Chapter 7

The Demonstration

The primary purpose of the **Demonstration Drive** is not to demonstrate the vehicle, but instead to get the prospect inside the dealership. Every selling step's primary purpose is to get to the next one. Pragmatists question the worth of anything that doesn't accomplish something. Remember "like outside...buy inside"? A secondary purpose is to determine whether "this vehicle is the one he likes." A major objective is for prospects (even those who don't buy) to leave from **inside** the building rather than outside.

*　　　　*　　　　*

Rules to Remember

1. Salesperson always drives first.

Why? Because he'll go on astonishingly more Demonstration Drives. It's an **Assumptive Demonstration.** The prospect isn't asked. The salesperson simply drives away with them as described in the previous chapter.

Practically no sales accrue without a Demonstration Drive. The most productive salesperson has the highest demo rate. Asking a prospect to go on a test ride has a high turndown rate. "Would you like to drive it?" asks the naive salesperson. "No. I've driven one." Rejection commences.

2. Decision-maker drives second.

Within several blocks, pull into a store-front parking area, get out, walk around the front of the vehicle to the passenger side, and open the front door.

Salesperson:

"It's your turn to drive, Henry. Hop out." (Command Phrase)

Henry follows salesperson to the driver's side, watches him move the seat rearward, gets in, buckles up, and accepts salesperson's direction about adjusting the seat. The child watches from directly behind with no fear of getting smunched. Salesperson seats himself in front passenger seat and buckles up.

Salesperson:

"Pull out onto the street, Henry, take a right, and stay in the right-hand lane. Not the next stoplight, but the one after that, turn right on Parkwater Boulevard."

The prospect doesn't know the route, so the salesperson must give directions well ahead of time to create a stress-free drive.

3. Right turns are preferred over left.

Safety and comfort are the reasons. Exceptions are one-way streets or driving in England and Australia. Left turns against on-coming traffic are unnecessary anxieties. Right turns are easier and safer.

4. Include a mid-point 'brochure shot' stop.

Factory brochures show vehicles in exotic and picturesque locations. Why not do the same during the Demonstration? Halfway through the preplanned route, stop at a scenic spot such as a park, playground or school campus.

Salesperson:

"Pull over there and stop, Henry. I want all of you to see something."

Henry does what he's told.

Salesperson:

"Turn off the engine, bring the key, and everyone follow me."

Prospects follow the salesperson out of the vehicle like a family of ducks to a spot about twenty-five feet away and admire the vehicle. When its the right vehicle, they begin to think of it as their own. Their comments reveal their likes and attitudes about it. Just one negative often means it's the wrong vehicle.

5. Non decision-maker drives third.

The 'brochure shot' stop is an excellent place to switch drivers to the Non decision-maker. If the Decision-maker asks to sit in front, the salesperson simply relates that company policy requires that the salesperson sit in front during test drives, "but here's your big chance to see for yourself how much leg room there is in the back seat…hop in."

6. Salesperson never sits in rear seat.

Front seating gives the salesperson control of the situation, whereas rear seating makes him a passive observer, who often can't overhear any conversation between the front occupants. Front seating allows the salesperson to engage each family member, maintain his matchup, direct the route, point out features and benefits, and be in the best possible position to assist the driver if there's an emergency.

7. Salesperson always goes on ride.

What good is the salesperson if he's not there? Don't even consider not going. Who better knows the idiosyncrasies of the vehicle and answers to queries? Unattended prospects have been known to purchase vehicles from other dealerships, who call afterward and request someone to get the vehicle off their lot. At Demonstration Drive's end, is the salesperson in a better position to get a prospect inside if he's with them...or not with them?

8. Follow preplanned route.

Using the same route allows the salesperson to concentrate on his prospect, the vehicle, and the matchup instead of where to go. It's safer, too, because if the vehicle malfunctions or runs out of gas, the dealership will know where to look. Try to avoid driving past other dealerships whenever possible One preplanned route is appropriate...with two adjuncts...depending on the type of vehicle and the age of the prospect. Generally speaking, elderly people prefer no traffic, slower speeds, and residential streets. The high-performance vehicle driver wants high-speed highways and curvy roads. The light pickup driver occasionally likes bumps and hills to climb.

9. Never ask how prospect likes vehicle, instead features and benefits.

The prospect may love the vehicle, but he doesn't want the salesperson to know, because he believes he'll lose some of his bargaining ability. So, if the salesperson asks, "How do you like it?", the prospect will give a cautious, wary, highly-qualified response followed by a question about price. Example:

Salesperson:

"How do you like it?"

Prospect:

"It's not bad. We've been looking around. It's more expensive than some of the others we've looked at. What's your best price on this one?"

If the salesperson answers directly, where will this prospect leave from when they return to the dealership…outside or inside? Outside, of course. He'll take the salesperson's verbal price to another dealership and ask if they can beat it. This occurs thousands of times daily throughout the country, much to dealers' chagrin. But, who caused the question about price? The salesperson! He asked the prospect how he liked the vehicle. Only the most unsophisticated prospect would do the following.

Salesperson:

"How do you like it?"

Prospect:

"It's just perfect. I can't believe we found just what we've been looking for."

Even though that may be true, most prospects have more sense than to reveal their likes before negotiations. Proper are questions about features and benefits. Truth bubbles to the surface. Keep track of 'likes' versus 'dislikes'.

Salesperson:

"How's the headroom back there, Henry?"

Susan:

"It's great. Our neighbor's car requires me to bend my head down when I ride in back."

Salesperson:

"I've got plenty of legroom up front. How about you?"

Henry:

"It's good. You can move the seat back farther if you like."

Salesperson:

"Not necessary. I've got extra room already. Susan, remember my telling you about the rack and pinion steering. Notice how responsive it is?"

Susan:

"There's no play in the wheel at all. Just like you said."

Salesperson:

"Don't turn your head toward me, Susan. Notice how much visibility you have all the way around because of the window design?"

Henry:

"Hey, that's right."

Salesperson:

"Like having eyes in back of your head. Looking straight ahead you can see all the important gauges...tachometer, odometer, temperature, oil pressure, high-beams, clock. Have you ever owned a dashboard so well-designed for the driver?"

Susan:

"Sure haven't."

10. Leave one question unanswered.

This subtle rule tests the prospect's willingness to go inside...without asking. When there's opposition, the salesperson has time to plan an alternate.

Susan:

"How big is the trunk?"

Salesperson:

"I'm not exactly sure. When we return to the dealership, we'll go inside and I'll get that information for you."

If the prospects say nothing, the salesperson knows that they know they're all going inside at Demonstration Drive's end.

11. Salesperson always drives back onto the lot.

If it's true that the driver is in control, then it follows that the salesperson must be driving at Demonstration Drive's end to improve the chances that the prospects will go inside. He can stop, park, open the door, and exit the vehicle at the proper moments. Several blocks from the dealership on the return trip, the salesperson should instruct the driver to pull into a predesignated area and stop.

Salesperson:

"Susan, at the end of the next block, pull onto that convenience store parking lot. Company policy requires that I drive back to the dealership. I think it keeps the insurance companies happy."

Citing company policy is a virtual tonic against debate. The prospect obeys and stops where commanded. The salesperson trades places with Susan and drives back to the dealership.

Bookend Speech

12. Invite inside with the "Bookend Speech."

A famous cosmetic ad campaign was headlined, "Does she...or doesn't she?" The question at Demonstration Drive's end is "Will they...or won't they go inside?" Everything that preceded it is geared to that objective. But it can't be accomplished before there's been a matchup between the prospect and the salesperson, dealership, and vehicle. When the salesperson believes those matchups have occurred, he eases the vehicle into a parking spot near the building entrance and relates the Bookend Speech.

"Susan, Henry, Josh, I'll tell you what. Why don't we make sure we have a complete description of this vehicle, with all the equipment on it and everything...we can go inside and do that, it won't take very long...and while we're doing that, I'm going to ask you to go ahead and describe your present vehicle. Follow me." He turns off the engine, opens his door, strides toward the dealership entrance, and holds the glass door open for them.

It's important that he give the foregoing speech while the vehicle is still moving. If he stops and turns off the engine beforehand, the prospects may get out first; and everything he does after that follows the prospects. Tilt.

The salesperson needs to lead the way. His exiting the vehicle first causes the prospects to follow him...odds improvement that they'll continue to follow him inside. The subtlety is microscopic...the result enormous. The request is the epitome of NonConfrontation...very prospect-friendly..."make sure we have a complete **description** of this vehicle". There's no trial close, no query about how they like the vehicle, no mention "if we can work out the right price, will you buy it today?", no "will this vehicle fit your needs?" None of those. Why? Because they trigger questions about price, discount, trade-in value, and interest rate. And once the prospect has those answers, he's prepared to depart and 'shop' those figures elsewhere. If it's possible to get prospects inside without those questions, isn't that preferable? What about the major objective for prospects to leave from inside the building rather than outside? The **Bookend Speech** question is disarming, since it preempts most prospects' claims to "want to shop around." How better than with a "complete description of this vehicle" for comparison purposes?

Bookend Speech gets its title from the illustration of two bookends holding up one book. The bookend on the left side represents the "description of this vehicle"; the bookend on the right side represents the "description of the prospect's present vehicle"; and the book is the statement, "go inside and do that." Many prospects consider the invitation to go inside scary. They have connotations of the rack, thumb screws, hot coals, beds of nails, a chamber of horrors. One reason is well-deserved...prior experiences of believing salespeople's promises made outside, then discovering they weren't true when they got inside.

The scary part c.) the invitation to go inside is bookended by two benefits, a.) a complete description of the newer vehicle, and b.) a description of the prospect's present vehicle. If the invitation to go inside is stated at the beginning of the sentence, the prospect can repel it before he even hears the rest, and the salesperson's explanation will sound defensive.

*   *   *

The wrong way:

The salesperson says, "Susan,Henry, Josh, I'll tell you what. Let's go inside and..."

"I'm not going inside," interrupts Henry, "until you tell me your best price."

"I thought we could get a complete description of this vehicle and..."

"I don't care about that until you tell me how much you're going to knock off the price."

"We could probably save you a couple of thousand dollars today."

"You've got to do a lot better than that."

*   *   *

Another wrong way:

"Susan, Henry, Josh," says the salesperson, "Let's go inside and..."

"Tell me your best price first," replies Henry.

"What's it going to take to earn your business today?"

"Just give me your bottom price, and I'll tell you if that's okay."

"What if I told you we could knock two thousand dollars off the price?"
"Get serious. I know you can do a lot better than that."

*   *   *

Another wrong way:

Salesperson eases into a parking place in front of the dealership, stops the engine, and turns to the prospects. "Well, Susan and Henry," he confides, "what do you think? Can we work something out to make you the proud owner of this vehicle today?"

"We've got to get to Josh's soccer practice right now," says Henry. "But, what's your best price? We want to look at a couple of other vehicles in the next week or so. We'll get back to you afterward if yours is the best price." The doomsday answer.

An excellent response is required at this critical time.

*   *   *

Willy Nilly Story

The salesperson says, "You know, Henry and Susan, the automobile industry has a problem that's not confined to this area. It occurs all over the country. Dealership employees quote figures and prices and trade-in values and rates and whatever. That may be okay, but the problem manifests itself when some customers who get this information don't do anything about it for a few days or a week or so or a month or more.

"Meanwhile, the vehicle that's being inquired about is sold to someone else. In the meantime the factory comes in with a price increase. In the meantime the customer's present vehicle is driven more, has more miles on it, is older, and is worth less. In the meantime the rates all change. Then the customer returns a few days later or in a week or so or a month or more and wants to hold the dealerships to those figures, which can't possibly work out.

"So, my boss has a policy that simply will not allow anyone to **Willy Nilly** quote any figures until two things occur. One, that the vehicle is one the customer has seen and driven and likes better than any other he's looked at; and two, that the customer is in a position to do something about the information right away.

"In this particular instance, neither of those are true of you. You've just said you wanted to look at other makes, and you just mentioned that you're not getting a vehicle right away. But one of the joys I have about working here is that we're never put into a position of telling customers things that ultimately cannot work out. It eliminates misrepresentations and any hard feelings with customers. I have an idea, though.

"For you to be an even smarter shopper, before you leave why don't we make sure we have a complete description of this vehicle so you can do a good comparison between it and any others you may choose to look at. It won't take very long. And while we're at it, we can get a description of your present vehicle. Follow me."

There's no reward to offer a discount outside, because the prospect will use the reduced price as a "shopping around figure" instead of going inside as he's implied.

Memorize the Bookend Speech and lead the way.

Salesperson:

a.) "Why don't we make sure we have a complete description of this vehicle, with all the equipment on it and everything. c.) We can go inside and do that, it won't take very long. b.) And while we're doing that, I'm going to ask you to go ahead and describe your present vehicle. Follow me."

And the sales process proceeds.

*   *   *

Recap

1. Salesperson always drives first.
2. Decision-maker drives second.

3. Right turns are preferred over left.
4. Include a mid-point 'brochure shot' stop.
5. Non decision-maker drives third.
6. Salesperson never sits in rear seat.
7. Salesperson always goes on ride.
8. Follow preplanned route.
9. Never ask how prospect likes vehicle, instead features and benefits.
10. Leave one question unanswered.
11 Salesperson always drives back onto the lot.
12. Invite inside with the Bookend Speech.

Chapter 8

Brief the Manager

Imagine what it would be like to attend a meeting where each individual spoke a different language. A busy dealership need not be the Tower of Babel. A sensible procedure to inform the sales manager about a selling situation follows the Demonstration Drive and assures a proper writeup procedure. Brief the manager is so important in the process that it has earned its own title as a selling step.

Salespeople get an adrenalin rush as they progress toward a sale and have a tendency to speed up. The good manager must slow them down. Salespeople believe that their transaction is the most important when several others are pending, but the manager can only be briefed one-at-a-time. Salespeople must omit personal opinions, because they're almost always wrong. Why? Because prospects give them erroneous information and visual clues.

Proof. If a prospect admits he won the lottery, will that help him get a lower price on a vehicle? If a prospect receives five thousand dollars from his grandmother for graduation, will that information help to reduce his down payment? If a bedraggled millionaire drives onto the lot in a twenty-five year old vehicle, will salespeople clamor to meet him? If he says he has no money, will others believe him? If a nephew drives his uncle's two year old Mercedes onto the lot, will he be treated differently than the aforementioned millionaire? Prospects are smart. Their most prevalent negotiation tactic is to act poor. Salespeople who are quick to believe are naive. That's fodder for personal opinions.

The salesperson brings the prospects inside from the Demonstration Drive, seats them at his desk, then enters the Manager's office, and writes information on the Description Board.

The salesperson begins his verbal briefing after the manager's acknowledgment.

"Go ahead, Andrew," says the Manager.

"I've just returned from the Demonstration with Bob and Mary Johnson," replies Andrew. "Bob is the principal driver. They're sitting at my desk. We drove Stock Number 4321, Year/Make/Model/Trim Level. The sticker price is eleven thousand two hundred eighty dollars. There's no additional equipment they'd like to add. They like it the way it is. Their present vehicle is a Year/Make/Model/Trim Level. I took a discreet look at it. The odometer shows fifty-one thousand some-odd miles on it. It's equipped with an automatic transmission, power seats both sides, power windows and locks, CD player, good tires, no broken glass, body looks good. No rust, dings or dents. It looks well-cared for."

The outline for the foregoing is always 1) Prospect's name, 2) Desired vehicle, and 3) Description of prospect's present vehicle. The manager doesn't need to worry about omissions and ask, "What year is it?" and "What's your prospect's last name?" and "Where are they now?" and "What's the stock number?" and "Do they want to add any equipment?" and "How many miles show on the odometer?", because the salesperson has already volunteered all of that information.

The salesperson's cursory knowledge of the prospect's present vehicle was obtained from two of the FBI Interrogation School Questions and a five-second walk-by. Merely walking past the vehicle and peering in the window provided his opportunity to read the odometer and scan the over-all physical condition. It's important that he not linger, as many prospects will believe he's appraising it. He's not. It will be appraised by the sales manager after the prospect makes a commitment to purchase the newer vehicle. If it's parked somewhere that's inconvenient for a Five-second walk-by, the salesperson will so inform the manager during the briefing.

The manager fills in the Date line and Stock Number line at the top of the Description as follows:

Date <u>4/21</u>
Stock No. <u>1234—1850PV—3850D—11280</u>

The Stock No. line always contains four separate numbers. The first number is the actual stock number. The second number is the pre-appraisal wholesale price for the prospect's present vehicle...followed by PV (prospect's vehicle). The third number is one-third down payment followed by the letter D (down payment). The fourth number is the selling price of the newer vehicle.

The second number should be approximately two hundred dollars below low wholesale book, because the vehicle hasn't been appraised yet, and there may be some anomalies and deficiencies that haven't been dis-closed or discovered. Additionally, the lowest possible price is mentioned initially, because a majority of vehicles that are traded in at dealerships are not retailed, but instead are sold to a wholesaler or taken to the auto auc-tion. Many franchised dealerships have a standard that requires a vehicle to be in excellent condition and below average mileage to be a candidate for retail resale, since the cost for reconditioning is prohibitive in many instances, and purchasers of late-model vehicles are as picky as those who buy new. Problem vehicles are anathema.

Even when the prospect has no vehicle to trade-in, there'll be a second number...0T for Zero Trade-in. The second and third numbers always end with 50 to standardize arithmetic problems that arise during the writeup procedure. After the manager has written the four numbers atop the Description, he'll ask questions to ascertain the 1) situation's level of difficulty; 2) quality of matchup; 3) quality of information; and 4) proper vehicle selection. Plus, he always desires to "slow the salesperson down, because adrenalin is pumping from the likelihood of a sale.

The Briefing continues.

"It sounds good, Andrew," says the Manager. "How you getting along with the Johnsons?"

"Real good," replies Andrew. "Bob knows someone at Hewlett-Packard who's my neighbor."

"Who will be driving the vehicle most?"

"Bob will."

"Will they be a two-car family?"

"Mary's got her own car, a three year old Nissan Maxima."

"Does she drive his car occasionally?"

"Sometimes. She's the one who said they wanted power seats on both sides and the CD player."

"Where do they live?"

"Up on 45th near the hospital."

"Just the two of them?"

"No. They have two boys who are at school right now."

"What school do they attend?"

"The oldest goes to Whitman Middle School. The youngest is at Emerson." The manager asks for information the salesperson has gleaned during his first selling step. The salesperson responds with no personal opinions. Nor has he uttered, "I don't know" or "I forgot to ask." No question concerns whether the prospects are committed. Remember the principle 'like outside, buy inside'.

So far, so good. The prospects like being there, like being with the salesperson, like the vehicle they've test-driven. The "buy" part still lies ahead.

"Was there any resistance when you invited them inside with the book-end speech?" asks the Manager.

"None," replies Andrew.

"Did you offer them a soda or coffee?"

"Yes. They accepted the first time I asked."

"Good. Here's the Description. Can you read the numbers?"

The numbers that the salesperson will mention first to the prospect are written beforehand on the Stock No. line.

"Yes," replies Andrew.

"See what you can do."

If the Manager had discovered that the prospects were 'resistant' to coming inside from the Demonstration Drive, or that they didn't accept the drink offer, he'd realize the situation might be challenging and be ready to assist. He's 'mentally inside this situation', and confident that the salesperson is well-prepared for the next step, the Description.

Chapter 9

The Description

_____ B.D. His_____ Hers_____

Date _____

Stock No. _____

DESCRIPTION

NAME		SALES
ADDRESS		SALES
CITY, STATE, ZIP		PHONE HOME
		PHONE WORK

☐ NEW	☐ USED	☐ CAR	☐ TRUCK		TRADE DATA		
YEAR	MAKE		MODEL	BODY	YEAR	MAKE		MODEL	BODY
COLOR		TRIM	MILES	COLOR		MILES	☐ Actual ☐ Unknown
STOCK #	VIN			VIN #			

SELLING PRICE

CUSTOMER'S VEHICLE

PAYOFF

DATE THRU

LIEN HOLDER

OFFICER

DOWN PAYMENT

* BANKS
ASK FOR
1/3 DOWN

TERMS

Although innocuous-looking, this potent document enhances the resources for a viable transaction, maintains the salesperson's control of the situation, and causes the prospect to volunteer important information.

Description is the appropriate name for it, because it describes the desired vehicle, the prospect's present vehicle, down payment, and terms. It's the first business document the prospect sees after being invited inside from the Demonstration Drive to get a "…complete description of this vehicle…" He sees what he'd been told he'd see. Informed and practiced use of the Description by the salesperson produces a higher selling price, lower trade-in value, more down payment cash, higher monthly payments, and shorter term than average…without confrontation with prospects who, ironically, enjoy the procedure.

Description dialogue allows the salesperson to get all the way down to the bottom box with little (if any) resistance from the prospect. A salesperson can become so adept with it that the prospect will seemingly be a graduate student of 'customer school' where he'd memorized the script, as he'll come in right on cue…ofttimes word-for-word.

Subsequent chapters include Description variations that include cash customers, prospects without trade-ins, price buyers, difference buyers, and subtleties of dialogue; but this chapter focuses on the most common situation…a prospect with a trade-in and an intention to finance.

General Principle: It is easier to make gross profit on a vehicle transaction when the prospect is worked on the monthly payment instead of the selling price.

The following dialogue follows the selling steps that lead to the Description, including the Greeting, Fact-finding, Presentation, Demonstration Drive, Brief the Manager, and the top half of the Description, which is filled out during the dialogue with the prospect just preceding this dialogue.

Salesperson:

"Mr. Johnson, the selling price of this vehicle is eleven thousand two hundred eighty dollars."

Prospect:

"That's way too much."

The prospect objected, because the salesperson stopped after one sentence and waited for his response. Suppose the salesperson had uttered two sentences before stopping?

Salesperson:

"Mr. Johnson, the selling price of this vehicle is eleven thousand two hundred eighty dollars. What's the selling price of your car?"

*   *   *

Dialogue in the First Box—Equipment

Most prospects believe that vehicle prices are outrageous. Dialogue that enables them to complain is counterproductive. Why not establish that two sales are occurring...a newer vehicle to the prospect...and the prospect's present vehicle to the dealership?

General Principle: The salesperson is not the Chairman-of-the-Board and must not act like he's responsible for any figures.

Given the two sentences in the prior dialogue, insert the foregoing general principle between them and it becomes:

Salesperson:

"Mr. Johnson, the selling price of this car is eleven thousand two hundred eighty dollars. Now I'm not the manager, Mr. Goodheart is the manager. And, I'm not the person who appraises vehicles, Mr. Goodheart does that too. But it's kind of a fluke. About a month ago we sold a car very similar to the one you're considering trading in, and as I recall, we sold that car for eighteen hundred fifty dollars. What is the selling price of your car?"

*   *   *

Dialogue in the Second Box—Customer's Present Vehicle

The Salesperson moves easily into the Second Box when he begins discussing the prospect's present vehicle. Notice the parallel language, sell...sell. Two sales are occurring concurrently. This irony provides the prospect, who believes the newer vehicle's price is outrageous, the opportunity to ask too much for his own. A second irony: His action of selling his present vehicle turns him into a buyer. Why would he desire to sell it if he didn't plan to replace it with another?

Prospect:

"That's ridiculous. My car's worth much more than eighteen hundred fifty dollars. I've got to get much more for it than that."

Salesperson:

"Yours must be a really nice one. What is the selling price of your car?"

Prospect:

"I don't know...but a lot more than that."

Most prospects know it's not wise to mention a figure first, that they should wait for the salesperson's figure hoping it'll be higher than they'd expected.

*   *   *

Mall Story

"Well, let me ask you this," says the salesperson. "I've got an idea. If you were to drive your present car over to the shopping mall, leave it there for a day or so, and put a great big 'for sale' sign in the window, what's the highest possible, the highest possible selling price you would write on that 'for sale' sign that you realistically believed you could sell your present car for? The highest possible?"

"I'd have to get at least three thousand dollars for it," replies the prospect.

"Three...three thousand dollars?" asks the salesperson. His eyes are wide.

"That's right."

The prospect aggressively attempts to sell his vehicle. The salesperson acts like a reluctant buyer. This is role reversal.

*   *   *

Redefine the Sign Story

"Excuse me, Mr. Johnson," says the salesperson, " but I believe I may have asked you the wrong question. I'm sorry. It's one thing to take your car to the shopping mall, leave it there for a day or two, and write a great big price on the 'for sale' sign. But what I should have asked instead is, what do you suppose you'd end up actually selling your car for? And, again, I'm really sorry for asking the question wrong. Will you accept my apology?"

"Yes." replies the prospect. "Well, I'd put three thousand dollars on the sign and probably end up taking twenty five hundred for it."

*   *   *

Cash Offer Story

"Wait," cautions the salesperson. "I've got another idea. Suppose your car sat over at the mall for more than a couple of days...let's say for a week or more. You'd do a back flip, Mr. Johnson, if you realized the large percentage of people who sometimes take several months to sell their vehicles. Anyway, suppose your car was parked there for a couple of weeks, and everyday after work you drove by to check on it. But nobody called…nobody left a note expressing any interest. So you finally decide that, well heck, now you've got to wash it, and you decide to move it to the shopping mall across town. And just as you were doing that, someone walked out of one of the stores, saw you, saw the car, saw the 'for sale' sign, then walked up to you and said, 'Hey, I'll buy your car, and I'll offer you cash.' What would you settle for under those circumstances…a totally hassle-free transaction?"

"Cash?" asks the prospect.

"Yes."

"Well, for cash I'd take twenty two fifty for it."

"Well, let me write that down. Yours must be a really nice one. I'll write it down like this." The salesperson says aloud what he writes down. "'Mr. Johnson would like…to try…to sell…his present vehicle'…for twenty two hundred fifty dollars?"

"Yes," replies the prospect.

"'For $2250…if possible,' "continues the salesperson. "By the way, Mr. Johnson, when you bought your present car, did you pay cash for it?"

This is a compliment, since it assumes the prospect has ready cash. The opposite, "Where did you finance your last car?" is uncomplimentary. Legitimate cash customers may be offended. No finance customer is offended by the assumption he's got money.

"No," replies the prospect. " I financed it."

"Oh, you mean you had monthly payments?"

"That's right."

"What were your payments all that time?"

"Two hundred ten dollars per month."

"Let me write that down. Two hundred ten dollars per month?"

"That's right."

"Okay. By the way, Mr. Johnson, do you have any remaining payments?"

"Yes. I still have six."

"Let me write that down. Six?"

"Yes."

"How do you know you still have six?"

"I have a payment coupon booklet from the bank. There are six coupons left."

"Okay. So then if you multiplied your two hundred ten monthly payment times six, you'd have a payoff of, let's see, six times zero is zero, six times one is six, six times two is twelve. It looks like twelve hundred sixty dollars. Does that sound right to you?"

"Yes, that sounds pretty close."

"Well, let me write that down. '$1260 according to Mr. Johnson.' By the way, whom do you make those payments to?"

"First National Bank."

"Let me write that down. Can you remember what city that branch is in?"

"Pasadena".

"Can you remember what street it's on?"

"Orange Grove and Colorado."

"Let me write that down. Can you recall who you talk to over there?"

"No. I just mail it in."

No hassle over the newer vehicle's selling price has occurred yet, but the salesperson has learned the prospect's selling price of his present vehicle, monthly payments, payoff, and lienholder.

*   *   *

Dialogue in the Third Box—Down Payment

"That's okay," continues the salesperson, "it doesn't make any difference. Mr. Johnson, the bank requires one-third down, and in this particular case, that would amount to a little bit less than thirty eight hundred fifty dollars. But, Mr. Johnson, if you go ahead and sell your present car for twenty two hundred fifty dollars like you're talking about, you're going to be in pretty good shape. Oh-oh. Wait a minute. No. You're going to be sixteen hundred dollars short. Oh, wait another minute. I almost forgot. You still owe twelve hundred sixty dollars on your present car. You'll be more short than that. Rats. You'll be short by twenty eight hundred sixty dollars. How were you planning on taking care of that, Mr. Johnson? By writing a check for twenty eight hundred sixty dollars? Or what was your plan in that regard?"

Arithmetic in 3rd Box

$3850	1/3rd down
-2250	his present vehicle
$1600	Short
+1260	Still Owing
$2860	Still Short

If the prospect gaped up at a piano falling on his head, he couldn't be more motivated to get out of the way. The fast growing down payment shortage has his entire focus, and he needs to act fast for fear it will grow larger. The salesperson wrote down the figures as he spoke them in the third box.

"I can't come up with twenty eight hundred sixty dollars for a down payment," responds the prospect. "I was hoping my present car would cover that."

"You'd need a tarp to do that," says the salesperson. "Only kidding. You know how these banks are, Mr. Johnson. They really like to see some cash for the down payment, regardless of your present car. What amount of cash can you come up with if you had to?"

"I can come up with a thousand or so, but not any twenty eight hundred."

"A thousand or so?" The salesperson sets down his pen atop the desk.

"Well, yes," answers the prospect.

"Will you be more specific?

"Well, when I say a thousand or so, maybe fifteen hundred, but that's all."

"Don't limit yourself. Fifteen hundred?"

"Yes."

"Realistically, Mr. Johnson, what are you really thinking?"

"Maybe a couple of hundred more."

"What would that make it?"

"Seventeen hundred."

"Well, let me write that down. Are you saying that you can come up with seventeen hundred for a down payment if you had to?"

"That's what I'm saying."

"Well, that's the way I'll write it down then. 'Mr. Johnson can come up with $1700...for down payment'...Mr. Johnson, I'm going to add 'if appropriate', how about that?"

"Fine."

"'If appropriate.' There. Let me read this part back to you to see if I wrote it down correctly. Can you see this?"

"Yes."

"Mr. Johnson can come up with seventeen hundred dollars for down payment if appropriate." Is that correct?"

"Yes."

"Okay." Salesperson rises from his chair and walks out, speaking as he exits. "Why don't you excuse me for a couple of minutes, Mr.Johnson, so that I can go in and see Mr. Goodheart, the manager, and based on these figures find out what your monthly payment will be. I'll be right back."

*   *   *

✓ B.D. His **7/4** Hers_____   Date _____ **11/06**_____

Stock No. **1234 - 1850 PV - 3850D - 11280**

DESCRIPTION

NAME Paul Johnson	SALES Andrew Fairweather
ADDRESS 8214 Huckleberry Lane	SALES
CITY, STATE, ZIP Santa Barbara, CA 93105	PHONE HOME (805) 555 - 6922
	PHONE WORK (805) 555 - 3000 Ext. 4

☒ NEW ☐ USED   ☒ CAR ☐ TRUCK   TRADE DATA

YEAR 2000	MAKE Toyota	MODEL Corolla	BODY 4 dr.	YEAR 1998	MAKE Ford		MODEL Tempo	BODY 4 dr.
COLOR Bermuda Blue metallic	TRIM DX	MILES		COLOR Gray		MILES 72,000 +		☐ Actual ☒ Unknown
STOCK # 1234	VIN			VIN #		according to Paul		

SELLING PRICE

Automatic   Cloth seats   11,280
AM/FM Stereo cassette   Tilt/Cruise
CD Player   Power windows
Alloy wheels   Air conditioning
Rear window defroster   Power seats

CUSTOMER'S VEHICLE

(1850)   Mr. Johnson would like to try
to sell his present vehicle for
$2250 if possible

PAYOFF	$210/mo X 6
DATE THRU	$1260 according to Mr. Johnson
LIEN HOLDER	
OFFICER	1st National Bank/Pasadena Orange Grove & Colorado

DOWN PAYMENT

Mr. Johnson can come up with
$1700 for down payment
if possible
appropriate.

```
  3850
- 2250
  1600
+ 1260
  2860
```

*BANKS
ASK FOR
1/3 DOWN

TERMS

The foregoing variation is referred to as a **Straight Line Description.** Everything the salesperson said was in a downward straight line to the bottom box. Verbiage in each box held the prospect's attention. Authorship for figures was attributed to others...the manager, the bank, the prospect. The salesperson at no time acted like the Chairman-of-the-Board. In the first box, he proudly stated the full retail price, but disclaimed responsibility for it by saying, "I'm not the manager, Mr. Goodheart is the manager." Not being confrontation's target is desirable. In each box, the numbers he'd mentioned first had been written on the stock number line during the Brief the Manager procedure by the manager.

Stock No.1234-1850PV-3850D-11280.
1234=Stock number
1850PV=Prospect's present vehicle
3850D=One-third down payment
11280=Retail price.

All others numbers were mentioned first by the prospect. In the second box, the prospect argued for negotiations for the selling price of his present vehicle, and he reduced his initial three thousand dollar selling price to twenty two hundred fifty dollars in response to the Mall Story, Redefine the Sign Story, and Cash Offer Story.

*   *   *

How the Numbers Decreased

$3,000	Customer's vehicle price after "Mall Story"
500	less after "Redefine the Sign Story"
$2,500	
250	less after "Cash Offer Story"
$2,250	Amount written down by salesperson in the Second Box.

*   *   *

Theoretically, the prospect may have reduced his price even further if he'd heard more stories. Some prospects mention a figure before the Mall Story. A few remain adamant about their first figure, although still arguing for negotiations. Even fewer don't volunteer a figure at all. They're usually non-buyers. Most blurt one out, though, in stunned, spasmodic rebuttal.

The third box is where the prospect becomes a buyer, because he's arguing for negotiation for monies required for the newer vehicle. Therein lies one of the vast differences between NonConfrontation Selling and other selling methods employed in retail selling. Incredibly, other philosophies require a buying commitment from the prospect before entering the building; but that leads to price reductions outside by salespeople, who must act like Chairmen-of-the-Board as they suggest discounts to bribed prospects. If a prospect will enter the building following the Demonstration Drive without being offered price reductions, isn't that preferable? Furthermore, where will a salesperson have more control over the selling situation and prospect,…outside or inside? And finally, when is negotiation more effective,…before or after the Greeting, Fact-finding, Presentation, and Demonstration Drive?

Only a few short minutes separate the end of the Demonstration Drive from the Third Box. Remember 'Like Outside…Buy Inside'? In the same way a chameleon transmutes from green to brown when he changes environment, so does the prospect turn from a 'liker' to a 'buyer' when he relocates from outside to inside. And moments later during the Description utters, "I can't come up with twenty eight hundred sixty dollars for a down payment. I was hoping my present car would cover the down payment." Can anyone maintain he's not arguing for negotiation?

Salesperson:

"You know how these banks are, Mr. Johnson. They really like to see some cash for the down payment, regardless of your present vehicle. What amount of cash can you come up with if you had to?"

Prospect:

"I can come up with a thousand or so, but not any twenty eight hundred and some."

What human being offers a one thousand dollar down payment when he's not buying anything? What's more, Mr. Johnson is speaking in the **present tense.** Not conditional or future tense. He's arguing for negotiation for the vehicle he's planning to buy **now.** The tense-change occurred during that particular exchange of dialogue. 'Could' became 'can'. And buyer-dom happened. Yet, the salesperson exited with no signed commitment to buy the vehicle. If he'd requested one, isn't it likely the prospect would have challenged the selling price?

Chapter 10

Preparing for the Commitment

Football is a game in which offense runs a play, then huddles around the quarterback to select the next one. Preparation and communication are the two principal reasons, although non-fans claim it is to give the players a rest.

The retail store has a quarterback...the duty sales manager. He's planned and participated in thousands of plays, yet his ability is limited by the quality of the information he receives from the salesperson. The Description serves as the prospect's x-rays. The mixed metaphor of sports and medicine is germane, because the sales manager must serve as the good doctor providing proper treatment and counsel for a healthy transaction, just as the quarterback must find a way to score touchdowns for a winning score.

Continuing the situation from the previous chapter, the salesperson completed the Description through the third box, then informed the prospect that he needed to "see Mr. Goodheart, the manager, and based on these figures find out what your monthly payment will be." The huddle commences. The manager's five objectives are: 1) determine whether it's a selling situation; 2) get mentally inside the transaction; 3) slow down the salesperson; 4) pencil a monthly payment in the fourth box; 5) authorize a credit application.

Not all completely filled-out Descriptions indicate selling situations. The prospect might not be the decision-maker. He may not have argued for negotiation. Perhaps the figures are the salesperson's, not the prospects. He may have spoken conditionally with 'woulds', 'ifs', 'whens' and 'maybes'. The described vehicle may lack desired equipment. Even though the decision-maker status may have been resolved during the Brief the Manager step, the prospect might have added information that changed it. Same with the described vehicle. The manager's job is to probe and determine.

"Did you tell me he's single?" asks the manager.

"Yes." replies Andrew.

"Will anyone else drive the vehicle?"

"No."

The decision-maker status is reconfirmed.

"Does the vehicle have any equipment missing that he said he'd like?" asks the manager.

"No. He likes it just the way it is."

The described vehicle is ready to deliver if sold. And, the prospect won't need to consult anyone before he buys.

"How did he arrive at twenty two fifty for his vehicle?" asks the manager.

"He started at three thousand after the Mall Story, went to twenty five hundred after the Redefine the Sign Story, then to twenty two fifty after the Cash Offer Story."

The manager knows now that the prospect argued for negotiation, and the figures are the prospect's, not the salesperson's.

"Does he know the loan officer?" asks the manager.

"He said he couldn't remember," says the salesperson. "He mails his payments."

The manager learns that the prospect has no finance preference.

"How did he arrive at the seventeen hundred dollars for the down payment?" asks the manager.

"When I showed him the twenty eight hundred dollar shortage," replies the salesperson, "he volunteered nothing at first claiming that his present vehicle equity should cover the down. Then he said 'a thousand or so' after I mentioned how banks like to see cash. When I asked him to be specific he increased to fifteen hundred. Slight tension caused another two hundred for the seventeen hundred."

The prospect argued for negotiation, and the figures are his, not the salesperson's. The manager carefully notes that the increases were one thousand, five hundred, and two hundred.

"Can you recall how he worded it?" continues the manager.

"When he went from zero to something, he said he 'can come up with a thousand or so'. He stayed in the present tense after that."

"Good. See if you can get him committed on this payment. Then fill out the credit application."

The manager pencils a monthly payment in the Fourth Box, and hands the Description and credit application to the salesperson. The salesperson knows the manager's high standards cause his own to be. He's become a world-class listener because the manager questions him about nuances and subtleties as esoteric as 'present tense' and the loan officer's name; is consistently demanding in his professional requirements; and has far surpassed the simpleminded 'how much?' and 'can you get more?' to 'how did he arrive at that figure?' and 'what words did he use?'. Further, the salesperson knows that the manager's discovery of the prospect's willingness to negotiate and subsequent transmutation into a buyer as he mentally gets inside the transaction mandates slowing the salesperson down to a pace that allows a nurturing attitude about transactions, and a strong belief that they develop rather than simply occur.

Chapter 11

The Commitment

Bambi Meets Godzilla

In the short film, "Bambi Meets Godzilla", the fictional deer romps in a sun-drenched, verdant meadow totally oblivious to the darkening sky. Dissonant music foreshadows imminent doom. Audience members shout warnings. Bambi looks up too late as Godzilla's massive, hairy foot crushes him flat. The end.

The film's length is less than two minutes. They meet!

When obtaining a **Commitment,** Bambi is the prospect. Godzilla is the villain…the bank. The salesperson's role is protecting Bambi from Godzilla, much like the audience screaming alerts at the screen during the film. Villains are disliked. The salesperson needs to avoid that title. So does the manager. Whomever the prospect thinks causes the monthly payment amount will be the villain. Why not hold out for a Hollywood ending?

The salesperson returns to the prospect from the manager's office with the Description and credit application in hand.

"Good news, Mr. Johnson," enthuses the salesperson. "Really good news. "You've just bought a car. Mr. Goodheart, the manager, said you can buy and drive this car home today…and for no more than the seventeen hundred dollars down payment that you already said you can do. I'm so pleased. Let me tell you everything he said."

The salesperson sits down as he continues his presentation without a pause.

"You can buy and drive this car home today," he bubbles. "The one with all the equipment on it that you said you want. The air-conditioning, AM/FM radio with the CD player and concert hall sound, power seats, sunroof, wire wheel covers, tilt wheel, cruise control, everything you want. He said he'd go ahead and buy your present car if you still want him to. He'll pay off the remaining balance you still owe to the bank. You won't have to be concerned about that anymore. He'll apply any equity to the transaction. And he said that, based on your good creditworthiness, he can do all this without any more cash for the down payment…just like you said you want. I'm really excited. However, in order for Mr. Goodheart, the manager, to be able to do all this, the bank, you know the bank, well the bank is going to require that your monthly payment be a little bit less than four hundred ten dollars per month. And in order to be able to do that, we're going to need some additional information…"

The monthly payment appears…just like Godzilla's foot…at the end and unexpectedly. But who causes it? The bank! The bank is Godzilla. The bank is the villain. The manager provides all the good things…the newer car with the desired equipment, he'll purchase the prospect's present car, pay it off, apply the equity, and not require more cash for a down payment. The solitary bad thing, the monthly payment, which is saved for last, is caused by the bank. Three times in one sentence the salesperson mentions 'the bank' to assure that the prospect knows who the villain is. Just as the sky darkened from Godzilla's bulk, so does the salesperson's demeanor change from upbeat to gloom. "I'm really excited," he'd related. "However, in order for Mr. Goodheart, the manager, to be able to do all this, the bank, you know the bank, well the bank is going to require that your monthly payment be a little bit less than four hundred ten dollars per month. And in order to be able to do that, we're going to need some additional information…"

The prospect is shocked when he hears the amount of the payment, then watches the salesperson focus on the credit application and begin to fill it out. This action must be stopped. It forces an immediate reaction from the prospect. Saying nothing implies his acceptance of the four hundred ten dollar monthly payment.

"Wait a minute," pleads the prospect. "Four hundred ten per month? I can't do that. I'm only paying two ten now. Maybe I can do two fifty, but not four ten."

"Two fifty?" responds the salesperson.

"Yes."

"Two fifty per month?"

"Yes."

"Well, let me ask you this, Mr. Johnson. What amount over and above the two fifty per month could you do **easily**?"

"None."

"I'm sorry, Mr. Johnson. I believe I asked you the wrong question. Sometimes I feel like such a goombah. Let me ask you this instead. I know nothing's easy. What if it was a little bit of a hardship? What amount over and above the two fifty per month could you manage, thinking about it that way?"

"Maybe ten or fifteen dollars."

"Mmm. Can you be more specific?"

"Look. I'll go two seventy-five, but that's it."

"Nothing's ever it, Mr. Johnson, but it does sound like you're trying to tell me that two seventy-five per month will be a lot **closer t**o what you can manage to do, is that correct?"

"A lot closer." The prospect resembles a deer caught in high beams.

"I'll write down whatever you want me to write down and go in and tell that to Mr. Goodheart, the manager, but before I do that, let me say this back to you to make sure I'm understanding you correctly. Is that all right?"

"Yes."

"Thank you. Wait. You do like the car we drove, don't you?"

"Yes."

"Well, that helps. So I think that what you're telling me is that if somehow, someway it can be arranged for the monthly payments to be around two seventy five per month...that's what it's going to take for you to buy and drive this new vehicle home today? Is that what you're trying to say?"

"You've got it right."

"Well, that's the way I'll write it down then, Mr. Johnson. Let's see. I know. I'll write it down this way." He says the text aloud as he writes it down. "'Mr. Johnson will buy and drive this car home today (now)...if somehow, someway the monthly payment is around $275 per month.' There! Let me read this back to you, Mr. Johnson, to make sure I've written it down the way you want me to. Then I'll go back and read it to Mr. Goodheart, the manager. This is what I wrote down. 'Mr. Johnson will buy and drive this car home today (now) if somehow, someway the monthly payment is around two hundred seventy five per month.' Did I write that down like you said, Mr. Johnson?"

"Yes."

"Good. So that Mr. Goodheart, the manager knows this is coming from you, why don't you okay it right here. Then I'm going to go back and actually read it to him."

Prospect signs it.

"And before I do even that," continues the salesperson, "we need some additional information."

Salesperson completes the credit application, obtains the prospect's signature on it, then exits to the manager's office with the committed Description and credit application in hand.

*   *   *

Outline

1. Headline
   A. Buy and drive the vehicle
   B. Down payment previously offered is okay
2. Buy and drive the vehicle...again
3. Equipment
4. We will buy prospect's vehicle
5. We will pay it off
6. We will apply the equity to the transaction
7. Down payment previously offered is okay...again
8. Godzilla's foot!
   A. The bank...the bank...the bank
   B. Required monthly payment
9. Stairstep to Commitment
   A. Closer...i.e. nearer to
   B. Verbal equals "if/buy"
   C. Written equals "buy/if"
10. Credit Application, then exit

Except for the Headline, numbers two through eight of the outline follow the four boxes of the Description. The Headline is exempted because it's the best of the good news offered in the dialogue, and most disarming. Most prospects plan to question the price, but when the salesperson returns and excitedly relates to him that he's just bought a vehicle for no more money than he'd previously volunteered for the down payment, the prospect opts to wait and hear the rest of the story.

*　　　　　*　　　　　*

Analysis of the Dialogue:

Salesperson:

Headline: "Good news, Mr. Johnson. Really good news. You've just bought a car. Mr. Goodheart, the manager, said you can buy and drive this car home today. And for no more than the seventeen hundred dollars down payment that you already said you can do. I'm so pleased. Let me tell you everything he said…"

If the salesperson quietly returns and sits down before he begins speaking, many prospects will control the situation by asking, "What's the price of the vehicle?" Hence, the salesperson must speak the headline **before** he sits down…and continue without waiting for any verbal acknowledgment.

Salesperson:

The First Box: "You can buy and drive this car home today, the one with all the equipment on it that you said you want. The air conditioning, AM/FM radio with the CD player and concert hall sound, power seats, sunroof, wire wheel covers, tilt wheel, cruise control, everything you want."

This is what the prospect will get for his hard-earned money. It's time for violins. In fact, bring out the entire orchestra. This is no place to short circuit. Then, a smooth transition into the second box.

The Second Box: "He said he'd go ahead and buy your present car if you still want him to. He'll pay off the remaining balance you still owe to the bank. You won't have to be concerned with that anymore. He'll apply any equity to the transaction."

So far, the prospect is getting all the benefit from this transaction. Nothing that he said he wanted has changed. Zero opposition. He's beginning to feel like a tubful of honey is being poured over him. Then, a smooth transition into the third box.

The Third Box: "And he said that, based on your good creditworthiness, he can do all this without any more cash for the down payment, just like you said you wanted. I'm really excited."

No acknowledgment from the prospect should be sought yet. Relating numbers two through seven of the aforementioned outline is tantamount to offering a sackful of gifts to the prospect. While gifts are being proffered from the sack, the prospect will say nothing....but instead be awestruck that there's no confrontation, that he's getting everything he asked for, that he's not being asked for more money, and that no figures have been changed, questioned, or challenged.

All of a sudden, we're in the fourth box.

The Fourth Box: "However, in order for Mr. Goodheart, the manager, to be able to do all this, the bank...you know the bank...well the bank is going to require that your monthly payment be a little bit less than four hundred ten dollars per month. And in order to be able to do that, we're going to need some additional information..."

Occasionally, a prospect is so stunned by the payment, he can't speak. It's important that the salesperson concentrate solely on the credit application until he does. When the salesperson asks, "How long have you lived at that address?" (an early question required by the credit application), the prospect will respond, "How much did you say the payment would be?" The salesperson **must** answer, "How little would you be short?" instead of repeating the amount of the payment. The text answer shows empathy, whereas the payment reiteration causes frustration and aggravation. Analysis of the dialogue continues.

Prospect:

"Wait a minute. Four hundred ten per month? I can't do that. I'm only paying two ten now. Maybe I can do two fifty, but not four ten."

Salesperson:

"Two fifty?"

Prospect:

"Yes."

Salesperson:

"Two fifty per month?"

Prospect:

"Yes."

Salesperson:

"Well, let me ask you this, Mr. Johnson. What amount over and above the two fifty per month could you do easily?"

$$*\qquad\qquad *\qquad\qquad *$$

Degree Questions

This is a **Degree Question**, very useful in negotiations. For example, one can utter, "Brrr, it's cold." But, how cold is it? And two people (one from Anchorage and the other from Tucson) will have entirely different interpretations. The Degree Question does not ask whether the prospect can pay more, because it's easy for him to say no. Instead, "what amount easily."

Prospect:

"None easily."

He doesn't say no, but implies the alternative.

Salesperson:

"I'm sorry. I believe I asked you the wrong question. Sometimes I feel like such a goombah. Let me ask you this instead. I know nothing's easy. What if it was a little bit of a hardship? What amount over and above the two fifty per month could you manage, thinking about it that way?"

Prospect:

"Maybe ten or fifteen dollars."

His two choices are something or nothing, but the odds for **something** are higher after a degree question.

Salesperson:

(gloomy) "Mmm. Can you be more specific?"

Another Degree Question. When a prospect offers a range...in this situation "ten or fifteen dollars", the salesperson errs if he grabs at the higher figure. The prospect will become wary and wonder to himself, "Why did he jump on the fifteen dollar figure and not the ten? All he cares about is my money. I've got to watch out for this person. No more volunteering. That's the last dollar he's getting out of me."

Prospect:

"Look. I'll go two seventy-five, but that's it."

*   *   *

Lock Language

Never write anything down immediately following **Lock Language,** because it will increase the difficulty for further negotiation later in the transaction. "That's it" is Lock Language, a verbal limit. And, just like taking air out of a balloon, the salesperson must stick a pin in it before proceeding.

Salesperson:

"Nothing's ever it, Mr. Johnson, but it does sound like you're trying to tell me that two seventy-five per month will be a lot closer to what you can manage to do, is that correct?"

Prospect:

"A lot closer."

*   *   *

Stairstep Commitment

CLOSER—(nearer to)
VERBAL = "If…Buy"____
WRITTEN = "Buy…If"

This staircase contains three step, Closer-Verbal-Written. The first step is always "Closer". Stairs cannot be skipped. The order never changes. But the salesperson may walk up and down them at will.

In the foregoing dialogue, the salesperson started down the stairs when he asked if two seventy-five per month was **Closer** to what the prospect could manage to do. How can the prospect say it's not closer? His only alternative is, "No, it's farther away." Of course it's closer to what he can pay compared to the four hundred ten dollars Godzilla's foot payment. He must say yes. Getting permission for the **Verbal** is next.

Salesperson:

"I'll write down whatever you want me to write down and go in and tell that to Mr. Goodheart, the manager, but before I do that, let me say this back to you to make sure I'm understanding you correctly. Is that all right?"

Prospect:

"Yes."

Salesperson:

"Thank you. Wait. You do like the car we drove, don't you?'

Prospect:

"Yes."

The 'Verbal' commences.

Salesperson:

"Well, that helps. So I think that what you're telling me is that **If** some-how,someway it can be arranged for the monthly payment to be around two seventy-five per month, that's what it's going to take for you to **Buy** and drive this new vehicle home today? Is that what you're trying to say?"

Prospect:

"You've got it right."

The Verbal requires If before Buy, because buy is a scary word and must first be conditioned by the payment amount.

Salesperson:

"Well, that's the way I'll write it down then, Mr. Johnson. Let's see. I know. I'll write it down this way."

The prospect's clear, affirmative, unambiguous response allows the salesperson to proceed to the Written, which he says aloud as he writes it in the fourth box.

Salesperson:

"'Mr. Johnson will buy and drive this car home today (now)…If somehow, someway the monthly payment is around…$275 per month.' There! Let me read this back to you, Mr. Johnson, to make sure I've written it down the way you want me to. Then I'll go back and read it to Mr. Goodheart, the manager. This is what I wrote down. 'Mr. Johnson will buy and drive this car home today (now) if somehow, someway the monthly payment is around two hundred seventy five per month.' Did I write that down like you said, Mr. Johnson?"

Prospect:

"Yes."

Salesperson:

"Good. So that Mr.Goodheart, the manager, knows this is coming from you, why don't you okay it right here. Then I'm going to go back and actually read it to him."

*   *   *

Penalty for Skipping or Inverting steps

1.__Skipping the Verbal.

The salesperson jumps from **Closer** to **Written**.

Salesperson:

"Nothing's ever it, Mr. Johnson, but it does sound like you're trying to tell me that two seventy-five per month will be a lot closer to what you can manage to do, is that correct?"

Prospect:

"A lot closer."

Salesperson:

"Well, that's the way I'll write it down then, Mr. Johnson. Let's see. I know. I'll write it down this way."

He says aloud the text as he writes it down.

Salesperson:

"'Mr. Johnson will buy and drive...'"

Prospect:

"Wait a minute! I didn't say I'd buy it. I just want to find out what the payment's gonna be!"

Rising temperatures cause lost sales. The prospect has every right to be upset, because he hasn't informed the salesperson that he'd buy it, which he might have done during the 'verbal' step; but the salesperson skipped it.

2.__Skipping the Verbal.

The salesperson appears too eager when he jumps from Closer to Written. There's no logical basis for the salesperson to sound eager about a two hundred seventy five dollar payment in response to the bank's four hundred ten dollar payment unless the bank's payment is not true or unless the salesperson knows that the lesser payment still earns a huge profit. The prospect will hate both of those possibilities. The Verbal step creates doubt, as the appropriate behavior from the salesperson is gloom and mild despair caused by a 'I don't think this will be possible' tone-of-voice.

Salesperson:

"Well, I'll write down whatever you want me to write down, and I'll go in and show it to Mr. Goodheart, the manager, but before I do that, let me say this back to you first. I want to be certain that I'm understanding you correctly. Is that all right?"

Prospect:

"Sure."

Salesperson:

"I think that what you're telling me is that if somehow, someway it can be arranged for the monthly payment to be around two seventy-five per month, that's what it's going to take for you to buy and drive this vehicle home today?"

The salesperson's countenance resembles that of a deer caught in high beams. How else can he act? If the bank payment is correct, the significantly lower payment offered by the prospect won't consummate a transaction, and everyone's time is wasted. Gloom is appropriate. Conversely, a salesperson's joy indicates that the lower payment will succeed, when in fact it won't.

3.__Inverting "If/Buy" to "Buy/If" during the Verbal.

Premature use of the word 'Buy' causes defensiveness.

Salesperson:

"I'll write down whatever you want me to write down and go in and tell that to Mr. Goodheart, the manager; but before I do, let me say this back to you to make sure I'm understanding you correctly. Is that all right?"

Prospect:

"Yes."

Salesperson:

"Thank you. Wait. You do like the car we drove, don't you?"

Prospect:

"Yes."

Salesperson:

"Well, that helps. So I think that what you're telling me is that you'll buy and drive this new vehicle home today if…"

Prospect:

(Angrily) "Not for any four ten per month."

Such a seemingly minor goof for such a major outburst. God created so many ways to do things. Which result is the salesperson's choice?

* * *

The Weasel

Many human attributes have animal names. Horse-sense, strong as an ox, meek as a mouse, memory of an elephant, stubborn as a mule, cowardly rabbit, eagle-eye, jackal, chicken, sly as a fox are just a few. Add **Weasel** to the jungle. A Weasel is a prospect who only sounds like he's committing. His escape route, **Weasel-talk,** says otherwise. Here are some examples:

"The monthly payment sounds okay, and I'll let you know in a couple of days."

"The fifteen thousand dollar selling price is lower than I thought it would be, but I want my father to see the truck, and he can't do that before Saturday."

"That's a deal. I'll do it, but I want my mechanic to look at the vehicle first."

All are variations of the same theme, **not right now, a condition is still pending.** Under no circumstances should a salesperson obtain a signed commitment when he's confronted with Weasel-Talk. A signed Weasel will claim that the dealership is committed to those figures, too; and if he returns as promised, he'll expect **no figures to change.** In Mr. Johnson's situation, has anyone appraised his present vehicle yet? No! Has anyone even looked at it? No! Won't that figure probably change when someone does? Yes! What about down payment cash? The monthly payment required by the bank was based on a seventeen hundred dollar down payment, but what additional amount will be required to support the prospect's desired monthly payment of two seventy-five? Bear in mind, that's one hundred thirty-five dollars less per month. The worst damage caused by committing a Weasel is his departure with what he considers to be the dealership's figures. He'll shop them all over town, asking competing dealerships to beat these figures. Conversely, if unsigned, he's leaving with **his own** figures, and no competing dealership can beat those. The Weasel reveals himself during the Verbal Stairstep when he hears the three separate words, **buy-today-now.**

Salesperson:

"It sounds like two seventy-five would be a lot closer to what you can manage. Is that right?"

Prospect:

"A lot closer. That's what I'm trying to tell you."

Salesperson:

"Well, I'll write down whatever you want me to write down and go in and tell that to Mr. Goodheart, the manager. But, before I do that, let me say this back to you to make sure I'm understanding you correctly. Is that all right?"

Prospect:

"Yes."

Salesperson:

"Thank you. Wait. You do like the car we drove, don't you?"

Prospect:

"Yes. I like it just fine."

Salesperson:

"Well, that helps. So I think that what you're telling me is that if some-how,someway it can be arranged for the monthly payments to be around two seventy-five, that's what it's going to take for you to buy and drive this new car home today now? Is that what you're trying to say?"

Prospect:

"Not today. I'm still looking around. But yes, the two seventy five payment sounds okay."

Classic Weasel-Talk. He likes the vehicle, he likes the payment, but not today. Without the Verbal, the salesperson may not find out until too late, after the prospect is out the door with what he considers to be the dealership's figures.

When the prospect is a Weasel, repeat the Verbal.

Salesperson:

"You know, I think I'm really understanding what you're trying to tell me, so let me say it back to you one more time just to be certain. Is that okay?"

Prospect:

"Sure."

Salesperson:

"Thank you. I think what you're saying is that, well, you do like the vehicle we looked at. In fact, you like it better than any other you've seen, and you're saying that if it can somehow, someway be worked out so that the monthly payment is around two seventy-five per month; and I am talking about the two seventy-five monthly payment, not that other one required by the bank. You're saying that if it can be worked out so that the monthly payment is around two seventy-five, that's what you're saying it is going to take for you to go ahead and buy and drive the car home today? Now do I have it right?"

Prospect:

"Yes, the payment is okay, but I still won't be able to let you know for sure for a couple of days."

The prospect remained a Weasel after the salesperson repeated the Verbal, hence the Salesperson must **Leave Without a Commitment.** Suppose the Weasel-talk went away after repeating the Verbal? Then the rule is, **Rerepeat the Verbal.** And if the Weasel-talk stays away, then write the **Commitment.**

Situation: Verbal…Weasel…Repeat Verbal…Weasel-talk goes away …Rerepeat Verbal…Weasel-talk stays away…Write Commitment. It commences at Closer step.

Salesperson:

"It sounds like two seventy-five would a lot closer to what you can manage. Is that right?"

Prospect:

"A lot closer. That's what I'm trying to tell you."

Permission for Verbal commences.

Salesperson:

"Well, I'll write down whatever you want me to write down and go in and tell that to Mr. Goodheart, the manager. But, before I do that, let me say this back to you to make sure I'm understanding you correctly. Is that all right?"

Prospect:

"Yes."

Salesperson:

"Thank you. Wait. You do like the car we drove, don't you?"

Prospect:

"Yes, I like it just fine."

Here comes the Verbal.

Salesperson:

"Well, that helps. So I think that what you're telling me is that if somehow,someway it can be arranged for the monthly payments to be around two seventy-five, that's what it's going to take for you to buy and drive this new car home today now. Is that what you're trying to say?"

The key words are stated without emphasis. Keep in mind, they're scary. The salesperson is walking on eggs.

Prospect:

"Not today, because I want my dad to see the car first, but the two seventy-five sounds okay."

Weasels are obvious when you know what to listen for.

Salesperson:

"You know, I think I'm really understanding what you're trying to tell me. Let me say it back to you one more time just to be certain. Is that okay?"

Prospect:

"Sure."

Now's the time to Repeat the Verbal.

Salesperson:

"Thank you. I think what you're saying is that, well, you do like the vehicle we looked at. In fact, you like it better than any other you've seen, and you're saying that if it can somehow, someway be worked out so that the monthly payment is around two seventy-five per month; and I am talking about the two seventy-five monthly payment, not that other payment required by the bank. You're saying that if it can be arranged for the monthly payment to be around two seventy-five, that's what you're saying it's going to take for you to go ahead and buy and drive the car home today? Now do I have it right?"

Prospect:

"Yes. Dad will like it. He doesn't need to see it. The payment is fine."

The Weasel goes away, so now it's time to Rerepeat the Verbal. After all that, the prospect has only said the payment's fine, not that he will buy the car and drive it home today. Great care is necessary. The eggs are still intact.

Salesperson:

"Well then, let me say it just one last time. You're saying, that if the monthly payment is two seventy-five per month, that's what it's going to take for you to buy and drive the car home today?"

Prospect:

"That's correct."

Salesperson:

"Let me write that down."

The salesperson must inform the manager that the prospect was a Weasel, and the basis for it. After all, regardless of what he said, the prospect may still be a Weasel.

Review of Weasel procedure:

1. When the prospect is a weasel, repeat the Verbal.
2. If the prospect remains a weasel, leave with no commitment.
3. If weasel-talk goes away after repeating the Verbal, rerepeat the Verbal.
4. If the weasel-talk stays away, write the Commitment.
5. Inform manager about weasel and basis for it.

*   *   *

Commitment Phrases

1. Always write the Commitment Phrase for a monthly payment in the Fourth Box of the Description.
2. Always write the Commitment Phrase for a selling price in the First Box of the Description.
3. Always write the Commitment Phrase for a Difference Price in the First Box of the Description.
4. Always write the Commitment Phrase for a down payment in the Third Box of the Description.

5. Wording for a Monthly Payment Commitment Phrase is: "Bob and Mary will buy and drive a newer vehicle home today (now) if somehow someway the monthly payment is around $375 per month."
6. Wording for a Selling Price Commitment Phrase is: "Bob and Mary will buy and drive a new vehicle home today (now) if somehow someway the selling price is around $15,000."
7. Wording for a Difference Price Commitment Phrase is: "Bob and Mary will buy and drive a new vehicle home today (now) if somehow someway the **Difference** between the selling price of the newer vehicle and the selling price of Bob and Mary's present vehicle is $8,000."

*　　　　　*　　　　　*

Horse Trader

Some prospects will not commit, regardless of how well the salesperson does his job. When the manager and salesperson are convinced that a selling situation exists, and that the prospect won't commit simply because he's adamant about having the dealership pencil the first figures and won't discuss any other subject until that occurs, then the following script may be considered.

Salesperson:

"I'm sorry this is taking so long, but Mr. Goodheart is working on this, and I've got to tell you that what you are asking him to do has put him into somewhat of a dilemma. You see, in order for Mr. Goodheart to do what you want him to do is going to require him to break a company policy. Let me explain what that company policy is. You see, when a customer comes to the dealership and finds a vehicle that he likes and is trying to work out the right arrangement to buy it, the company policy is one whereby the manager is not supposed to know that the customer is serious about wanting to buy the vehicle until **after** the customer has made some kind of offer to buy it, regardless of how good or bad that offer is. And of course, in this case you have not done that. And that is the dilemma facing Mr. Goodheart right now. That's what is taking him so long. I did tell him very emphatically that that is what you wanted him to do. At the same time, I told him something about you that I totally believe, and I would like you to consider it to be a personal compliment. May I tell you what I told Mr. Goodheart about you?

Prospect:

Sure.

Salesperson:

Thank you. I told Mr. Goodheart, and I truly hope you find no offense in this, because I absolutely intended it as a compliment, that the reason you were insisting on this is because, well, because you are the **Horse Trader** type. Do you find that offensive?

Prospect:

No.

Salesperson:

Thank you. I appreciate that. Well, as soon as I mentioned that to Mr. Goodheart, a magic lightbulb seemed to turn on and glow over his head. He brightened up, and he said, 'Well, that changes everything!' He also said that he respects that, he appreciates that, and that he would honor that. And, if that is the thing that is impeding progress in this particular situation, he said he would get the ball rolling anyway. So, let me tell you what he said. Mr. Goodheart said, 'Well fine.' That means you can go ahead and get this vehicle, the nice new one with all the equipment you want on it such as the tape deck, the power seats, the angry looking tires with the alloy wheels, the five-speed transmission, and all the other things that you like on it. He said we would still go ahead and buy your present vehicle, if you want us to. We will pay off the remaining balance, you don't need to worry about that anymore. And he said he would get the ball rolling, anyway, so that you will know that we are making the first offer anyway. So regardless of how much or how little it seems to you, you can get this vehicle today, and he has worked out the price, just to get the ball rolling of $11,220. So do you want to go ahead and show Mr. Goodheart that you really are the Horse Trader type or not?

At this moment, the prospect will exclaim greatly or make a counteroffer…usually the latter.

Prospect:

"What? That's only $60 off!"

Salesperson:

"Well, he did abide by your wishes and made the first offer. He got the ball rolling, anyway, and he didn't have to break a company policy to do it. How little of that amount would you be lacking?"

Prospect:

"You tell him that I wouldn't pay a dime more than $9500."

Now, into the **Commitment** mode. Not all prospects will respond with an offer, but it's another way to go to improve the odds of obtaining an offer without giving away the gross profit to do so.

Chapter 12

Price Buyer

The **Price Buyer** is anathema to many salespeople. His mantras are, "What's your best price?" and "How much will you knock off?" That salespeople cause prospects to become Price Buyers by highlighting price and discount from the get-go is an irony many don't overcome. Additionally, commission salespeople, who are paid a percentage of the gross profit, arrange their own paycheck deductions when they're quick to discount or talk price. During the Description, the Price Buyer constantly asks about price. He's easy to detect.

*   *   *

The Procedure

1. Commit the prospect to a price in the First Box.
2. Complete the Description through the Third Box.
3. Disclose the requested discount.

4. Add the requested discount to the selling price of prospect's present vehicle.
5. Make prospect's offer ridiculous.

*   *   *

First, let's examine how simple it is to ignore the mantras. The numbers in the Stock No. line atop the Description for this example are: 1234-7850T-6950D-19780

The salesperson fills out the Description in front of the prospect through the ten features in the Equipment Box...and continues as follows:"Mr. Mallis," recites the salesperson, "the selling price of this truck is nineteen thousand seven hundred eighty dollars. Now I'm not the manager, Mr. Goodheart is the manager. And, I'm not the person who appraises vehicles, Mr. Goodheart does that too. But it's kind of a fluke. About a month ago we sold a truck very similar to the one you're considering trading in, and as I recall, we sold that truck for seven thousand eight hundred-fifty dollars. What is the selling price of your truck?"

"It had to be a toilet," replied Mr. Mallis. "My truck's worth twice that."

Even though the prospect wants to be a Price Buyer, he can only do and think about one thing at a time. His need to defend the price of his present vehicle is his first priority.

"Yours must be a really nice one," replies the salesperson. "What is the selling price of your car?"

"Eleven thousand dollars," says Mr. Mallis airily. "Look at what you're asking for yours."

His first attack. The salesperson chooses to ignore it.

*   *   *

The Mall Story:

"Well, let me ask you this," says the salesperson. "I've got an idea. If you were to drive your present truck over to the shopping mall, leave it there for a day or so, and put a great big 'for sale' sign in the window, what's the highest possible selling price you would write on that 'for sale' sign that you realistically believed you could sell your present truck for? The highest possible?"

"That doesn't make any difference," replies Mr. Mallis. " What kind of discount am I going to get on the new one? That's what's important!"

His second attack. The salesperson suspects he may have a serious Price Buyer on his hands, but his standard is for three attacks to occur before launching the Price Buyer procedure.

"I hear what you're saying," replies the salesperson, "and I can appreciate how important that is to you; but first let me finish this up. What would be the highest possible selling price you'd put on a 'for sale' sign that you realistically believed you could sell your present truck for. The highest possible?"

The salesperson acknowledges the price question, stays on his straight line dialogue, and asks his own selling price question.

"I've seen trucks like mine advertised for more than eleven grand in the paper."

"Eleven thousand dollars?"

"That's right."

The prospect responds to the salesperson, not vice-versa. A Price Buyer is defined as one who stays in the First Box of the Description. That's where the Selling Price is. If he doesn't, he's not a Price Buyer, although he may sound like one.

*   *   *

Redefine the Sign Story:

"Excuse me," continues the salesperson, "but I believe I may have asked the wrong question. It's one thing to take your truck to the shopping mall, leave it there for a day or two, and write a great big price on the 'for sale' sign. But what I should have asked instead is, what do you suppose you'd end up actually selling your car for? And, again, I'm really sorry for asking the question wrong. Will you accept my apology?"

"Yes," responds Mr. Mallis. "Well, I'd put eleven thousand dollars on the sign and probably end up taking ten thousand for it. What are you going to do about **your** price?"

His third attack. It's decision-time for the salesperson, who can continue down to the bottom box...or commence the 5-step procedure for a Price Buyer. In this example, he chooses the latter.

*   *   *

1. Commit prospect to a price in the first box.

"Well, you have picked out the brand new MAKE/MODEL" says the salesperson, "the one with the 5-speed transmission, cloth seats, four wheel drive, air conditioning, AM/FM radio with the CD player, bed liner, special oversized tires, and the selling price of that vehicle is nineteen thousand seven hundred-eighty dollars. And if you have a different figure than that in mind, I'll go ahead and write it down and go in and tell that to Mr. Goodheart, the manager. So what figure, if any, would you like me to write down? But you have picked out the brand new MAKE/MODEL, the one with the 5-speed transmission, cloth seats, 4-wheel drive..."

"Look," interrupts Mr. Mallis. "I'll give you sixteen-five for it."

Mallis responds to a **Broken Record,** a three-part, drone-like monotone that's repeated over and over unceasingly until the prospect blurts out a price. Then there are two beats of silence...the reward for his cooperation.

"Sixteen five?" says the salesperson.

"Sixteen thousand five hundred dollars," responds Mr. Mallis.

"I wished you'd told me this earlier," says the salesperson with a gloomy tone. "I could have shown you one of those other trucks without so much equipment, and a couple of years older."

"I want this one. I know you guys can discount."

"Well, let me ask you this, Mr. Mallis, making it as easy on yourself as possible, what amount over and above the sixteen thousand five hundred dollars can you do, thinking about it that way?"

"Let's see if the sixteen five works?"

"It sounds like sixteen five is a lot closer to what you have in mind."

The **Stairstep Commitment** commences with the First Step…Closer.

"Absolutely," demands Mr. Mallis.

The salesperson knows it's time to obtain permission for the **Verbal.**

"I'll write down whatever you want me to write down," says the salesperson, "and go in and tell that to Mr. Goodheart, the manager, but before I do that, let me say this back to you to make sure I'm understanding you correctly. Is that all right?"

"Yes."

"Thank you. Wait! You do like the truck we drove, don't you?"

"Yes."

Verbal time. Notice how the word "**If**" precedes the word "**Buy**".

"Well, that helps," says the salesperson. "So I think that what you're telling me is that **If** somehow, someway it can be arranged for the selling price to be around sixteen thousand five hundred…that's what it's going to take for you to **Buy** and drive this new truck home today? Is that what you're trying to say?"

"You've got it right."

"Well, that's the way I'll write it down then. Let's see. I know. I'll write it down this way."

The salesperson says the text aloud for the Commitment as he writes it down. Notice how the word "**Buy**" precedes "**If**", the exact opposite of the Verbal .

"'Mr. Mallis will buy and drive this new truck home today (now)…if somehow, someway the selling price is around $16,500.' There! Let me read this back to you to make sure I've written it down the way you want me to. Then I'll go back and read it to Mr. Goodheart. This is what I wrote down. 'Mr. Mallis will **Buy** and drive a new truck home today (now) **If** somehow, someway the selling price is around sixteen thousand five hundred dollars.' Did I write that down like you said?"

"Yes."

"Good. So that Mr. Goodheart, the manager, knows this is coming from you, why don't you okay it right here. Then I'm going to go back and actually read it to him."

Prospect signs it.

*　　　　*　　　　*

2. Complete Description through the third box.

The continuation commences at the precise point that was interrupted by the price commitment.

"Before I read this to Mr. Goodheart," says the salesperson, "I want to clarify something we've been talking about. Remember you told me that you'd like to try to sell your present truck for ten thousand dollars, regardless of what amount you'd write on a 'for sale' sign after you left it parked at the mall for a couple of days?"

"Yes," replies Mallis.

*　　　　*　　　　*

The Cash Offer Story

"Suppose," says the salesperson, "your truck sat over at the mall for more than a couple of days, let's say for a week or more. You'd do a back flip if you realized the large percentage of people who sometimes take several months to sell their vehicles. Anyway, suppose your truck was parked there for a couple of weeks, and everyday after work you drove by to check on it. But nobody called, nobody left a note expressing any interest. So you finally decide that, well heck, now you've got to wash it, and you decide to move it to the shopping mall across town. And just as you were doing that, someone walked out of one of the stores, saw you, saw the truck, saw the 'for sale' sign, then walked up to you and said, 'Hey, I'll buy your truck, and I'll offer you cash.' What would you settle for under those circumstances…a totally hassle-free transaction?"

"For cash I'd take ninety-five hundred," replies Mallis.

"Ninety-five hundred dollars?"

"Yes."

"Well, let me write that down." The salesperson says the text aloud as he writes it down. " 'Mr. Mallis would like to try to sell his present truck…for $9500 if possible.' By the way, I can't remember if I asked whether or not you said you paid cash for your present truck."

"I make payments."

"What are your payments?"

"Four forty five per month."

"Let me write that down. Four forty five?"

"Yes.

"Okay. Do you still have any?"

"Yes. I have fifteen left."

"Let me write that down. Fifteen?"

"Yes."

"How do you know you still have fifteen?"

"I counted the payment coupons when I made my most recent payment."

"So then if you multiplied your four hundred forty-five dollar monthly payment times fifteen, you'd have a payoff of, let's see, it looks like six thousand six hundred seventy five dollars. Does that sound right?"

"Yes, that sounds pretty close."

"Well, let me write that down. '$6,675 according to Mr. Mallis.' By the way, whom do you make those payments to?"

"Acme Credit Union."

"Let me write that down. What street are they on?"

"State Street."

"Let me write that down. Can you recall who you talk to over there?"

"Yes. Mrs. Butterfield."

"Let me write that down. Now Mr. Mallis, the bank requires one-third down, and in this particular case, that would amount to a little bit less than sixty nine hundred fifty dollars. But, Mr. Mallis, if you go ahead and sell your present truck for ninety five hundred dollars like you're talking about, you're going to be in pretty good shape. Oh-oh. Wait a minute. You still owe sixty six hundred seventy-five dollars on your present truck. You're going to be short by forty one hundred twenty five dollars. How were you planning on taking care of that, Mr. Mallis? By writing a check for forty one hundred twenty five dollars? Or what was your plan in that regard?"

Salesperson writes down the figures as he speaks them.

Arithmetic Problem in Third Box

> $6,950 Down Payment
> -9,500 **Amount Mr. Mallis wants for his present truck**
> $2,550 **Credit**
> $6,675 **Still Owing on Mr. Mallis' truck**
> $4,125 **Shortage**

"I thought my equity would handle the down," replies Mallis. "It did last time I bought a vehicle."

"The fly in the ointment is your payoff," says the salesperson. "What portion of that can you pay off?"

"I haven't made this month's payment yet. It's coming due."

"You mean apply that?"

"Yes."

"I see. That won't change it much. What would it amount to, though?"

"Five hundred dollars?"

"I see. Putting that thought aside for a moment and getting back to the down payment shortage, what portion of just that amount could you manage easily?"

"None. Well maybe a couple of hundred."

"I guess every little bit helps, but the question is, will it help enough? A couple of hundred for the down payment added to five hundred or so toward the payoff would amount to about what?"

"Seven hundred?"

"Well, even if we're not successful working this out, I want to thank you for trying so hard to think of ways to help."

The salesperson sets down his pen and slowly turns over the Description. He resembles Sherlock Holmes trying to solve a case, frustrated by his inability. Five to ten seconds elapse.

"I don't suppose you have any other thoughts?" says the salesperson."Look," replies Mallis, "I'll come up with an even twelve hundred. That's more than I…"

"Mr. Mallis," interrupts the salesperson, "I promised I'd write down whatever it is you want me to write down, and if you want me to write down twelve hundred dollars, I will. Do you?"

"Yes."

"Let me write that down. 'Mr. Mallis can come up with $1200 for down payment if appropriate.' There! Let me read this part back to you to see if I wrote it down correctly. Can you see this?"

"Yes."

The salesperson reads the Description phrase to him. " 'Mr. Mallis can come up with twelve hundred dollars for down payment if appropriate.' Is that correct?"

"Yes."

The Description is complete through the Third Box. However, since the prospect has already signed a commitment, the salesperson won't exit yet to "find out what the monthly payment will be," but will instead accomplish the remaining three steps of the Price Buyer Procedure, which are 3) Disclose the requested discount; 4) Add the requested discount to the selling price of prospect's present vehicle; and 5) Make the prospect's offer ridiculous.

*   *   *

3. Disclose the requested discount.

Although subjective, a discount's size can appear unreasonable to some prospects who might question its legitimacy. Guilt plays differently to each. Many aren't aware of its enormity until it stares back at them.

"Before I go in and read this to Mr. Goodheart," says the salesperson, "I want to show you how he's going to look at it. Even though the regular selling price of the new truck is nineteen thousand seven hundred eighty dollars, you've said you want to pay right around sixteen thousand five hundred, isn't that correct?"

"Yes," replies Mallis.

"Well, if you subtract sixteen thousand five hundred from nineteen thousand seven hundred eighty dollars, what you're actually asking for is, good grief, you're asking for a discount of thirty two hundred eighty dollars. Do you realize that?"

Arithmetic Problem

$$\begin{array}{r} \$19{,}780 \\ \underline{-16{,}500} \\ \$\ 3{,}280 \end{array}$$

"Sure," replies Mallis.

"Well, now's a good time to change it before I show it to him," says the salesperson. "Really. What would you like for me to change it to?"

"I don't want to change it. Let's see what he says."

*   *   *

4. Add requested discount to the selling price of his present vehicle.

"Well, okay, but that's how he's going to look at it. Remember how you'd told me that you'd like to try to sell your present truck for ninety five hundred dollars?"

"Yes."

"The way Mr. Goodheart, the manager, is going to look at this, you really don't want to try to sell your truck for ninety five hundred dollars. Do you realize that?"

"What?"

"You want to try to sell your truck for ninety-five hundred dollars, **plus** the three thousand two hundred eighty dollar requested discount for a total of twelve thousand, seven hundred eighty dollars. That's the way Mr. Goodheart is going to look at it. I just want to make certain you understand it that way."

Arithmetic Problem

$ 9,500 Amount Mr. Mallis wants for his present truck
+<u>3,280</u> Plus Requested Discount
$12,780 Present Truck Plus Discount

"He can look at it however he wants to," replies Mallis. He looks stunned.

"Let me show you **why** he's going to look at it that way so that you can appreciate what he'll be trying to working out," says the salesperson. "Remember you said that you wanted to pay sixteen thousand five hundred for the new truck?"

"Yes."

"And you originally said that you wanted to try to sell your present truck for ninety-five hundred dollars? Isn't that right?"

"Yes."

"Well, if you subtract the ninety five hundred from the sixteen thousand five hundred, that makes a difference of seven thousand dollars. Can you see that?"

Arithmetic Problem

$16,500 Price Offered for New Truck by Mr. Mallis
-9,500 Amount Mr. Mallis wants for his present truck
$ 7,000 Difference

"Yes." Mallis stares at the figures.

"Well, the reason that Mr. Goodheart, the manager, is going to look at it that way is because the selling price of the truck is actually nineteen thousand seven hundred eighty dollars. And he's going to see that you want to sell your present truck for twelve thousand seven hundred-eighty dollars. When he subtracts it, the difference is seven thousand dollars. **Same difference.** Can you see the reason now?"

Arithmetic Problem

$19,780 Selling Price of New Truck
-12,780 Present truck plus discount
$ 7,000 Same difference

"I guess so," says Mallis.

Diagram of Same Difference

$19,780 Regular Selling Price	$16,500 Prospect's Offer
-12,780 Present truck + discount	9,500 Present truck
$ 7,000 Difference	$ 7,000 Difference

"Do you still want me to show this to Mr. Goodheart?" asks the salesperson.

"Sure," replies Mallis.

*   *   *

5. Make his offer ridiculous.

The salesperson stands up and looks at the Description. "Fine," he says. "You do like this truck, the one with all the equipment, the one we drove. And even though you originally said you'd like to try to sell your present truck for ninety five hundred dollars, it appears you really want twelve thousand seven hundred eighty for it. If I were you, I don't know that I'd get my hopes up. But wish me luck."

Chapter 13

Cash Customer

The **Cash Customer's** focus is on price. Every last nickel of it is coming out his pocket today, thus he's motivated to wage a fierce struggle for it during negotiations. Many disdain the process, as do a majority of sellers.

In English-speaking countries, negotiation is a lost art. It's uncommon. Most consumers do not bargain over the cost of food, and toys, and household goods, and clothing, and hardware, and personal computers, and membership fees, and sporting goods, and gasoline, and office supplies, and theater tickets, and books, and jewelry, and medicine, and lawn mowers, and cosmetics and hundreds of thousands of products and services that pervade the marketplace. Conversely, in the Middle East, Asia, South America, and Southern Europe, negotiation is commonplace…even for a loaf of bread.

Logically, the salesperson should be the professional negotiator, since he deals with hundreds of situations each year; whereas the prospect is the amateur, who negotiates once every three or four years for a newer vehicle, but not for most other products and services that he purchases. Albeit, a

146

prospect's limited tactics of bluster, ambivalence, and intimidation often succeed in drastically reducing the price.

Many tactics revealed in this chapter are not exclusive to cash customer situations.

*   *   *

Outline of Procedure

1. Prospect must persuade salesperson that he really is a **Cash Customer**.
2. Leave with no commitment.
3. Rare
4. Rare…again.
5. Dinky discount.
6. Commitment
7. Disclose the requested discount.
8. Rare…a third time.
9. Second Dinky discount.
10. Looking for a 'Willingness to Negotiate'.

*   *   *

The following prospect has no vehicle to trade in. The second box is crossed out. Notice that the second figure on the stock number line is 0T, indicating no trade-in.

Stock No. 1235- 0T-8650D-25655

"Mr. Chipps," says the salesperson, "the selling price of this vehicle is twenty-five thousand six hundred fifty five dollars. Now, I'm not the manager, Mr. Goodheart is the manager. Oh, by the way, the bank requires one-third down, and in this particular case that would amount to a little bit less than eighty six hundred fifty dollars…"

"Wait a minute," interrupts Mr. Chipps. "I told you before that I'm paying cash!"

"That's right! Let me ask you this, Mr. Chipps. **What bank are you getting the cash from?**"

"First National."

"Then your plan is to make monthly payments to the First National Bank?"

"That's right."

The prospect plans to finance his vehicle, not pay cash. Answering the question, "What bank are you getting the cash from?" removes his mask. Some prospects are advised by financial institutions to **act** like a cash customer, obtain the figures, then retreat to the bank for the loan. A downside of that tactic from the seller's point-of-view is that the prospect shops the final figures at competing dealerships. The prospect would need to prevaricate to evade the 'what bank' question.

Starting again with a legitimate cash customer.

"Mr. Chipps," says the salesperson, "the selling price of this vehicle is twenty five thousand six hundred fifty five dollars. Now, I'm not the manager, Mr. Goodheart is the manager. Oh, by the way, the bank requires one-third down, and in this particular case that would amount to a little bit less than eighty-six hundred fifty dollars..."

"Wait a minute," interrupts Mr. Chipps. "I told you before that I'm paying cash!"

"That's right! Let me ask you this, Mr. Chipps. What bank are you getting the cash from?"

*   *   *

1. Prospect must persuade salesperson that he really is a Cash Customer.

"None," replies Mr. Chipps. "It's **my** cash. I'm paying cash."

"Cash?," repeats the salesperson. "It's so seldom that I meet someone with cash to pay for a vehicle."

"That's what I'm telling you."

"Let me write that down. You mean you're cashing in a CD or something?"

"It's in my savings account. I'm going to write a check on it."

"A local savings account, Mr.Chipps?"

"Hermitage Credit Union."

"Let me write that down."

"I'm not going to pay that much, though. How much will you knock off?"

"Just a moment, Mr. Chipps. Let me finish writing this last part down." The salesperson says aloud what he's writing down. " 'Mr. Chipps will be paying cash for the car, and he will be writing a check on his savings account at Hermitage Credit Union.' What branch?"

"Downtown."

"Let me write that down. 'Downtown branch.' Can you recall what street?"

"Foster at Kenmore."

*   *   *

2. Leave with no commitment.

"Mm. 'Foster at Kenmore.' Mr. Chipps? I need to check something with Mr. Goodheart. I'll be back."

The salesperson exits. He's completed the first two steps. Mr. Chipps persuaded him that he really **is** a cash customer. The salesperson **Left with No Commitment.** If he'd asked for one, a price challenge would have ensued, and the opportunity to build value by making the vehicle rare would be lost.

*   *   *

3. Rare

In the same way that a kitten is tantalized by a dangling piece of string it can't quite reach, so is a prospect's desire for a vehicle that's in short supply. He knows whether or not he loves it, but for him to retain any bargaining position he must **act like he doesn't.** His action of reaching out for it belies his masquerade.

The salesperson returns holding nothing in his hands. "Mr. Chipps," he says, "Mr. Goodheart is working on the figures. He'll be just a few minutes. I thought, why wait in his office and possibly cause him to take longer, when I can wait here and keep you company? Is that all right?"

"That's fine," replies Mr. Chipps.

"Thanks. By the way, he made a suggestion that will allow you to help him out. You'll undoubtedly find it somewhat strange. May I just blurt it out?"

"What is it?"

"Well, the vehicle that we've been looking at, the one we described with all the equipment you want and everything, the one that's Bermuda Blue...?"

"What about it?"

"Mr. Goodheart wondered if you'd consider one very similar to it, but a different color. And before you say anything, I admit it sounds strange, let me tell you why he wondered that. I don't know how you managed to do it, Mr. Chipps, but you've actually picked out the vehicle with the equipment, the style, the model, and the color that everyone in the country seems to want. Out of dozens of vehicles in inventory, you've cherry-picked **the car!** The center out of the Danish. You may not know this, but the most popular and most hard-to-get vehicles can ofttimes not be ordered from the factory. They're practically impossible to obtain. The factory has a strict allocation on the best-sellers. They **ship** those vehicles to the dealerships. We don't know they're coming until they arrive. Here's the problem. Even though there might be fifteen exactly the same at the factory, there are hundreds of dealerships all over the country clamoring to get one. Consequently, only one dealership in a two or three state area may actually receive one. It's not quite as bad as I make it sound, though, because each dealership has a computer like ours in their office. We enter code numbers that enable us to know the inventory at the other dealerships. They know ours too, of course. Anyway, this vehicle's recent arrival showed up on everybody's computer. Triggering inquiries. I know that Mr. Goodheart, will do whatever it takes to work everything out for you. We've got several other vehicles in stock similar to this one. He wondered if you'd at least consider a different color than Bermuda Blue. That would make it much easier for him to work out a good price for you. Will you?"

"No. This is the one I want."

The salesperson's effort to **take the vehicle away** from Mr. Chipps is thwarted. No longer can the prospect **act** disinterested. His overt action to obtain it by spurning other choices has taken off his mask. He's a fervent buyer. The value of his heart's desire skyrocketed while his bargaining power plummeted.

An irony is that Mr. Chipps doesn't want to make it easy for the manager to work out a good price, because he wants this vehicle. Conversely, a "Yes" determines he's looking at the wrong vehicle, as evidenced by his not reaching out for the piece of string; and it can be followed by an effort to present a different vehicle that's not so easy to take away from him. Even the largest dealerships normally don't stock two vehicles exactly alike. The plethora of models, trim levels, and special packages make it difficult to even have one of each.

"Mm," says the salesperson. His funereal countenance complements his gloom. "Well let me ask you, Mr. Chipps, what at least would be your second choice?"

"I don't have a second choice. This is the one."

The salesperson tugs, but the prospects grasps it firmly.

"I was afraid you'd say that," says the salesperson. "Mr. Goodheart won't be happy to hear this."

"I don't care."

Pour irony from a syrup jug.

"Let me try this, Mr. Chipps," asks the salesperson. "Suppose that God Himself did not even invent Bermuda Blue? What color would you have chosen instead?"

"Sorry." Mr. Chipps crosses his arms and sits back in his chair.
"Is that your final answer?"
"My final answer."

*   *   *

4. Rare...Again.

Saying something twice not only reinforces it, but increases its credibility. An ideal thought in the prospect's mind after the salesperson walks to the manager's office is, 'There's no way they're going to take this vehicle away from me. Heh heh heh." This very short presentation is simply for that purpose.

The salesperson returns to his own office and stands in the doorway. "Mr. Chipps? Mr. Goodheart needs one more minute. Have you thought about a different color?"

"No."

"I told Mr. Goodheart you'd probably say that, but it doesn't hurt to ask. I'll be back."

Selling occurs while the prospect sits alone. 'They really **do** want me to consider a different vehicle,' he thinks. 'I'm not going to. I've got their best one and I'm going to keep it.'

*   *   *

5. Dinky Discount

The basic premise that 'the prospect never likes the first price' is carved in stone. He never likes the first **anything!** That includes payment, interest rate, trade-in allowance, and discount. Once the salesperson accepts that premise, he knows the prospect's response to a proffered discount will **always** be negative, regardless of whether it's for fifty dollars or five hundred dollars or one thousand dollars or two thousand dollars or whatever. Zero exceptions exist amongst sane prospects to this universal truth.

Rare must always precede **Dinky Discount,** as it establishes the seller's motive for proffering such a lilliputian price reduction, and elevates the prospect's conscious desire for the vehicle. Albeit, the prospect still won't like a Dinky Discount, but disparate emotions of bewilderment and desire will render him incapable of stifling a price rejoinder of his own.

"Good news, Mr. Chipps," says the salesperson as he returns from the manager's office with the Description in hand. "Mr. Goodheart has worked this out on the Bermuda Blue vehicle, not another color. as you insisted. He said he could see no reason why you can't buy and drive this car home today. the one with all the equipment on it that you said you want. The air conditioning, AM/FM radio with the CD player and concert hall sound, power seats, sunroof, wire wheel covers, tilt wheel, cruise control, everything you want. And yes, like I said, it is the Bermuda Blue one. Mr. Goodheart said that car is yours. I hope you're pleased. And, he said that even though the regular selling price of the car is twenty five thousand six hundred fifty five dollars, you can buy it and drive it home today for twenty five thousand six five hundred ninety dollars. And in order to be able to do that, I'm going to need some additional infor…"

"Wait a minute," interrupts Mr. Chipps. "What? That's ridiculous! Sixty dollars off? I'm thinking about paying twenty three thousand for it".

He can't restrain himself. His commitment blurts out as involuntarily as a hiccup.

*   *   *

6. Commitment

"That's why I kept asking if you'd at least consider a different color," says the salesperson. "I know that Mr. Goodheart will do practically anything price-wise to sell some of the other vehicles we have. You just happened to pick out the one that everybody wants. This hasn't been easy for him. Twenty-three thousand dollars? Realistically, Mr. Chipps, what are you really thinking? We are talking about the Bermuda Blue one."

"That's what I am really thinking," responds Mr. Chipps. "Twenty three thousand. I'm paying cash!"

"Mr. Chipps. Making it as easy upon yourself as possible, what amount over and above twenty three thousand could you do...thinking about it that way?"

"Maybe five hundred, but my gosh."

"What would that make it?"

"Twenty three thousand five hundred."

"Mm." The salesperson is the picture of dejection. "Let me ask you this, Mr. Chipps. What if it wasn't so easy? In fact, I'm sorry I asked you the question that way. What if it was a bit of a struggle? What amount over and above the twenty three thousand five hundred could you do? I wish things weren't so difficult."

"Twenty three five is more than I was planning on."

"What would you like me to tell Mr. Goodheart?"

"Tell him I can go to twenty three thousand seven fifty."

Stairstep Commitment Commencing with Closer

CLOSER—(nearer to)
      VERBAL = "If...Buy"____
           WRITTEN = "Buy...If"

"Mm," replies the salesperson. "That would be closer to what you can afford than that other figure that Mr. Goodheart wrote down?"

"Yes."

Permission For the Verbal

"I'll write down whatever you want me to write down and go in and show it to Mr. Goodheart, but before I do, let me say it back to you to make sure I'm understanding you correctly. Is that all right?"

"Yes."

"Thank you. Wait. You do like the car we drove, don't you?"

"Yes."

Verbal—"If/Buy"

"Well, that helps," says the salesperson. "So I think that what you're telling me is that **If** somehow, someway it can be arranged for the selling price to be twenty three thousand seven hundred fifty dollars instead of the twenty five thousand six hundred and something figure, that's what it's going to take for you anyway to **Buy** and drive this new vehicle home today? Is that what you're trying to say?"

"You've got it right."

"Well, that's the way I'll write it down."

Written—"Buy/If"

The salesperson says the text aloud as he writes it down. " 'Mr. Chipps will **Buy** and drive a car home today (now) **If** somehow, someway the selling price is around $23,750.' There! Let me read this back to you to make sure I've written it down the way you want me to. Then I'll go back and read it to Mr. Goodheart. This is what I wrote down. 'Mr. Chipps will buy and drive a car home today (now) if somehow, someway the selling price is around $23,750.' Did I write it down like you said?"

"Yes."

"Good. So that Mr. Goodheart knows this is coming from you, why don't you okay it right here? Then I'm going to go back and actually read it to him."

Prospect signs it.

"And before I do even that," says the salesperson as he gazes at the signed Description and sets a credit application down on the desk in front of him, "we need some additional information."

Obtaining a partial credit application (5-liner) for a Cash Customer is appropriate and necessary to verify that adequate funds exist for the transaction. Normally, the information is limited to name, address, birth date, social security number, and signature. When accomplished, then:

*   *   *

7. Disclose the Requested Discount

Although subjective, a discount's size can appear unreasonable to some prospects who might question its legitimacy. Guilt plays differently to each. Many aren't aware of its enormity until it stares back at them.

"Before I go in and read this to Mr. Goodheart," says the salesperson, "I want to show you how he's going to look at it. Even though the regular selling price of the new car is twenty-five thousand six hundred fifty five dollars, you've said you'll pay twenty three thousand seven hundred fifty dollars, isn't that correct?" "Yes," replies Mr. Chipps.

"Well, if you subtract twenty three thousand seven hundred fifty from twenty five thousand six hundred fifty five dollars, what you're actually asking for is, good grief, you're asking for a discount of one thousand nine hundred and five dollars. Do you realize that?"

"Sure."

Arithmetic for Discount

> $25655 OK $25590 (less $65)
> -<u>23750</u> customer's offer
> $ 1905 disclosed discount

"Now's a good time to change it before I see him," says the salesperson. "What should I change it to?"

"Leave it alone," replies Mr. Chipps. "See what he says."

"Will do. Let's see. You do like this car, the one with all the nice equipment that you like, the one we drove, the Bermuda Blue one. Even though the regular price is twenty five thousand six hundred fifty five dollars, you're saying you'll pay twenty three thousand seven hundred fifty dollars, a discount of one thousand nine hundred and five dollars. I don't know that I'd get my hopes up if I were you, Mr. Chipps, but I'm going to show it to him anyway. Wish me luck."

*   *   *

8. Rare…a Third Time.

Testing the prospect's resolve for the vehicle, much like a doctor checking a patient's vital signs, is a precursor for a high-probability, profit-improvement sortie. The prospect's desire for the vehicle must outweigh its cost. This short presentation is similar to the previous **Rare** step.

*   *   *

9. Second Dinky Discount.

Consider the illogic of offering a large discount now. Wouldn't the prospect wonder that if this vehicle is so rare and so popular and so in demand and so hard-to-get, why a big price reduction? Doesn't logic instead require that the price **not** be lowered for those reasons? Albeit, it's imperative to show the prospect a seller's willingness to negotiate (since arrogance is not appealing); and it must precede the buyer's. Hence, a **Second Dinky Discount** of less than sixty dollars is proffered. The reader must ask himself what size discount won't the prospect object to? The answer is "none." Even a vehicle offered absolutely free of charge would elicit, "What's wrong with it?" At least in the prospect's mind.

Huge discounts have dominated retail selling practices for decades only to be confronted with, "You're got to do better than that" by adamant prospects. Sellers offer rewards for **non-cooperation** in the form of further price reductions. Why not rewards for **cooperation?** Once prospects know that resistance will be rewarded, what's their motive to stop? The Dinky Discount only works, though, after the prospect won't allow the vehicle to be taken away from him. Rare must always be the precedent.

*   *   *

10. Looking for a 'Willingness to Negotiate'.

The prospect must be willing to increase his offer **by at least the same amount as the seller is willing to reduce his price.** That defines **'Willingness to Negotiate'**, the goal for the **Second Dinky Discount.** If the seller reduces his price by fifty dollars, for example, the prospect must be willing to increase his offer by at least fifty dollars. Without the dollar match or more, there's no 'Willingness to Negotiate,' and the transaction stops in place.

The following principle is one of the most amazing in this book. **The prospect's 'willingness to negotiate' is typically six to ten times greater than the seller's.** Translation: When the prospect responds to a fifty dollar discount, he improves his offer by three to five hundred dollars or more...not simply fifty! An applicable descriptive slogan is, "Give a little...get a lot."

Conversely, when the seller reduces his price by hundreds of dollars, the prospect improves his offer by only a fraction. The applicable replacement slogan becomes a cause for business failure, "Give a lot...get very little."

The range for **Dinky Discount** is between fifty and sixty-five dollars.

Showing the Figures

$ 25655 OK $25590 (less $65)	$25590
-23750 customer's offer	-25530
$ 1905 disclosed discount	

The salesperson returns to the prospect with the Description in hand. "Mr. Chipps. Mr. Goodheart has worked this out, sorry it took him so long, but before I show it to you, I want to let you know that I wish I'd done a better job of talking you into a vehicle that was closer to your price range; but in that regard, I've convinced Mr. Goodheart, much to his dismay, that you wouldn't consider it. So, let me show you what he's done. He said, 'Okay, if that's the only vehicle you'll consider,' the Bermuda Blue one with all the nice equipment that you want, even though the regular price is twenty five thousand six hundred fifty five dollars, you can buy it and drive it home today for twenty five thousand, five hundred thirty dollars. So what, if anything, would you like me to tell Mr. Goodheart in that regard?"

The prospect gapes in disbelief. Unseen forces cause his mouth to move and words to spill out in the same way that pounding a tube of toothpaste with the cap off causes a big squirt.

"I'm a cash customer," he blurts. "I can't believe it! That's less than a hundred dollars. Look, you tell him I'll pay twenty-four thousand five hundred, and that's all."

His two choices were to offer something or nothing. 'Something' amounts to seven hundred fifty dollars. Not bad for a procedure that added less than four minutes to the selling time. Any amount he offered from zero to forty nine dollars would not have met the definition of **'Willingness to Negotiate'**, and the transaction would come to a screeching halt.

Chapter 14

Difference Buyer

Even though a **Difference Buyer** has no concept of the four Description boxes or the rationale for keeping them separated, he's inadvertently jamming the first two boxes together and causing one figure to emerge...the Difference between the selling price of the new vehicle and the selling price of the prospect's present vehicle. The basic strategy for dealing with a Difference Buyer is to separate the two jammed together boxes.

Subtracting the prospect's present vehicle value from the newer vehicle's selling price results in the Difference price.

Example:

$20,000 Selling Price of newer vehicle
-<u>15,000</u> Trade-in allowance
$ 5,000 Difference Price

The 5-Step Procedure

1. Commit in the top box.
2. Complete Description through the third box.
3. Subtract the Difference from the Selling Price.
4. Disclose the two Selling Prices of the prospect's vehicle.
5. Make prospect's vehicle Selling Price ridiculous.

Ironically, **Difference Buyers** are created by salespeople and sales managers, who'd rather deal with one number than two. Once the Difference Buyer has a Difference Price shown to him, he uses it for his shopping around figure.

"How much Difference do I have to pay?" he asks menacingly at each subsequent dealership.

The salesperson briefs the manager that he's got a Difference Buyer. "Oh, one of those," responds the manager, as though a Difference Buyer were one of God's aberrations. Then, during the Description in the first box:

"Mr. Johnson," recites the salesperson, "the selling price of this car is nineteen thousand nine hundred eighty-five dollars. Now I'm not the manager, Mr. Goodheart is the manager. And, I'm not the person who appraises vehicles, Mr. Goodheart does that too. But it's kind of a fluke. About a month ago we sold a car very similar to the one you're considering trading in, and as I recall we sold that car for five thousand six hundred fifty dollars. What is the selling price of your car?""I don't care about that," replies Mr. Johnson. "I'll pay a difference of ten thousand dollars."

"Oh-oh. You used a word I'm not absolutely certain about. What do you mean...'difference?'"

"I mean I'll buy your car and trade mine in, if I don't have to pay more than ten thousand dollars **Difference**."

"I see what you're saying, Mr. Johnson. Let me say it back to you so you know that I understand. You're telling me that regardless of what the selling price of the newer vehicle is...and regardless of what the selling price of your present vehicle is...you'll buy the newer vehicle and trade in your present vehicle, so long as what you refer to as the **Difference** is ten thousand dollars? Is that what you mean?"

"Precisely."

"I see. Well, let me ask you this, Mr. Johnson, making it as easy upon yourself as possible, what amount over and above the ten thousand dollar **Difference** can you manage, thinking about it that way?"

"None. I'm telling you ten thousand dollars. Period."

*   *   *

1. Commit in the top box.

"I see. Mm. You do like the vehicle that we drove, don't you?"

"Yes"

"I'll write down whatever it is that you want me to write down, but before I write anything down, let me say this back to you first to be sure I have it correct. Is that all right?"

"Yes."

"You're saying that if somehow, someway it can be worked out so that what you refer to as the **Difference** between the selling price of the newer vehicle and the selling price of your present vehicle is ten thousand dollars, that's what you're saying you'll do to buy and drive this vehicle home today? Did I say that right?"

"Yes."

"Well, that's the way I'm going to write it down then. 'Mr. Johnson will buy and drive a newer vehicle home today now if somehow someway the **Difference** between the selling price of the newer vehicle and the selling price of his present vehicle is around $10,000.' Is it okay if I use the word 'around', Mr. Johnson?"

"So long as it's right around."

"Thank you. There! Let me read this back to you. Can you see this all right?"

"Yes.

The salesperson reads aloud the Commitment Phrase. " 'Mr. Johnson will buy and drive a newer vehicle home today now if somehow…someway the **Difference** between the selling price of the newer vehicle and the selling price of his present vehicle is around $10,000.' Okay?"

"Good."

"Why don't you okay it right there so that Mr. Goodheart knows this is coming from you instead of something I made up?"

Prospect signs the Commitment. The words 'Selling Price' are written twice in the Commitment Phrase. That's important in order to separate the Difference into two figures at procedure's end.

*   *   *

2. Complete Description through the third box.

"Before I take this in to Mr. Goodheart," says the salesperson, "I want to complete filling this out. Remember a few minutes ago I mentioned that we'd sold a vehicle similar to yours a couple of weeks ago for five thousand six hundred fifty dollars? Pretending for a moment that you weren't going to replace it with another vehicle, what would be the selling price of your car?"

"I was thinking around seventy five hundred dollars," replies the prospect.

*   *   *

The Mall Story

"Well, let me ask you this, Mr. Johnson," queries the salesperson. "I've got an idea. If you were to drive your present car over to the shopping mall, leave it there for a day or so, and put a great big 'for sale' sign in the window, what's the highest possible, the high possible selling price you would write on that 'for sale' sign that you realistically believed you could sell your present car for? The highest possible?"

"At least seven thousand dollars."

"Seven thousand dollars?"

"That's right."

The prospect aggressively attempts to sell his vehicle. The salesperson acts like a reluctant buyer. This is role reversal.

*   *   *

The Redefine the Sign Story

"Excuse me, Mr. Johnson," says the salesperson, "but I believe I may have asked you the wrong question. I'm sorry. It's one thing to take your car to the shopping mall, leave it there for a day or two, and write a great big price on the 'for sale' sign. But what I should have asked instead is, what do you suppose you'd end up actually selling your car **for?** And, again, I'm really sorry for asking the question wrong. Will you accept my apology?"

"Yes," replies the prospect. "Well, I'd write seven thousand dollars on the sign and probably end up taking sixty five hundred for it."

*   *   *

The Cash Offer Story

"Wait. I've got another idea," replies the salesperson. "Suppose your car sat over at the mall for more than a couple of days, let's say for a week or more. You'd do a back flip, Mr. Johnson, if you realized the large percentage of people who sometimes take several months to sell their vehicles. Anyway, suppose your car was parked there for a couple of weeks, and everyday after work you drove by to check on it. But nobody called, nobody left a note expressing any interest. So you finally decide that, well heck, now you've got to wash it, and you decide to move it to the shopping mall across town. And just as you were doing that, someone walked out of one of the stores, saw you, saw your car, saw the 'for sale' sign, then walked up to you and said, 'Hey, I'll buy your car, and I'll offer you cash.' What would you settle for under those circumstances, a total hassle-free transaction?"

"Cash?"

"Yes."

"Well, for cash I'd take sixty two fifty for it."

"Well, let me write that down. Yours must be a really nice one. I'll write it down like this. 'Mr. Johnson would like to try to sell his present vehicle' for $6250?"

"Yes."

"'For $6250 if possible.' By the way, Mr. Johnson, did you pay cash for it?"

"No, I financed it."

"Oh, you mean you had monthly payments?"

"That's right."

"What were your payments all that time?"

"Three hundred sixty dollars per month."

"Let me write that down. Three hundred sixty dollars per month?"

"That's right."

"Okay. By the way, Mr. Johnson, do you have any remaining payments?"

"No. It's paid for."

"Let me write that down. Mr. Johnson, the bank requires one-third down, and in this particular case, that would amount to a little bit less than sixty eight hundred fifty dollars. But, Mr. Johnson, if you go ahead and sell your present car for sixty two hundred fifty dollars like you're talking about, you're going to be in pretty good shape. Oh-oh. Wait a minute. No. You're going to be six hundred dollars short. How were were you planning on taking care of that, Mr. Johnson? By writing a check for six hundred dollars? Or what was your plan in that regard?"

Arithmetic Problem

$ 6,850 Down Payment

<u>-6,250</u> **Amount Mr. Mallis wants for his present truck**

$ 600 **Shortage**

"Nothing down," replies the prospect. " My trade-in should handle it nicely."

"You know how these credit unions and banks are," says the salesperson. They really like to see some cash. What amount of cash for a down payment could you come up with you had to."

"I won't have to. I'm sticking to zero."

"It sounds like you'd prefer to come up with zero cash for the down payment."

"Now you're talking."

"Let me write it down that way. 'Mr. Johnson would much prefer to come up with…zero cash for down payment if appropriate.' "

*   *   *

3.   Subtract the Difference from Selling Price.

With a Straight Line Description, the salesperson would exit at the end of the third box to "find out what the monthly payment will be." But, the Difference Buyer is already committed in the top box, and the procedure requires returning there to separate the Difference figure into two separate selling prices.

"Before I take this to Mr. Goodheart, I want to show you how he's going to look at this. Even though the regular selling price of this vehicle is nineteen thousand nine hundred eighty five dollars, you're saying that you'll buy and drive the car home today for what you call a Difference of ten thousand dollars. Is that correct?"

"Yes."

"When we subtract the ten thousand dollar Difference from the regular price, it reveals that you want to sell your present vehicle for nine thousand nine hundred eighty five dollars. Can you see that?"

The Arithmetic

  $ 19,985 Regular Selling Price
  -10,000 Difference
  $ 9,985 Amount Mr. Mallis wants for his present truck

"Yes," replies the prospect.

*   *   *

4.   Disclose the two selling prices of his vehicle.

"Wait a minute," says the salesperson. "Look at this. Down here we wrote that you 'want to try to sell your present vehicle for six thousand two hundred fifty dollars.' Which is it? It's got to be the same in both places. What do you want me to tell Mr. Goodheart about this? He's bound to ask."

Such a paradox. The prospect needs to explain his inconsistency to the salesperson. $9985 vs. $6250 for the same vehicle? What is the price? He has two choices…1) increase the $6250 in the second box to $9985; or 2) reduce the $9985 in the top box to $6250. Either choice reveals he has no predetermined price for his present vehicle. He's being wishy-washy. His desired Difference figure has no relationship to the worth of his present vehicle. All prospects know that, except the mentally deranged. The salesperson must act indifferent about which figure the prospect changes. Most will opt to increase the second box figure. The salesperson simply crosses out the $6250 and replaces it with $9985, which, of course, makes the selling price of the prospect's present vehicle ridiculous. Even the prospect knows he won't sell it for that much.

*   *   *

5.   Make his selling price ridiculous.

"Well, tell him I'm only paying a Difference of ten thousand dollars," replies the prospect. "So I guess that means you should change the $6250 to $9985."

"Good thing I asked before I showed this Mr. Goodheart," says the salesperson. "I'll just cross out the $6250 and write in $9985. Like this. At least it's not two different figures now. Do you still want me to show this to him?"

"Sure."

The salesperson stands up holding the Description and looking disconsolate.

"Okay, I will. You want to buy and drive this car home today. And originally you said you wanted to try to sell your present vehicle for $6250, but now, all of a sudden you want to sell it for $9985. I don't know if I'd get my hopes up if I were you, Mr. Johnson, but I promised you I'd show it to him, and I will."

The salesperson exits.

Chapter 15

Valuating the Trade

No one places a higher value on depreciable personal property than its current owner, and a prospect with a vehicle to trade in is no exception. He has no qualms about overpricing his, because he believes that dealerships overprice theirs; and he knows that a higher trade-in value will reduce his desired vehicle's down payment, monthly payment and amount to finance.

When others show interest in his present vehicle, his asking price increases; when not…it plummets if he truly intends to sell it. This is the basic tenet of supply and demand. He keeps secret his antipathy for the vehicle, but his sanguine testimony regarding its performance, reliability, and low maintenance cost is ofttimes misrepresentative.

Suppose his true confession was extracted? And that his words and actions exposed his real motivation regarding his vehicle? Its overt rejection by him is the goal of valuating the trade.

Many prospects determine their selling price by scanning the classified ads for similar vehicles. Some affix 'for sale' signs to the window hoping for an offer. Others do nothing more than ask a friend or co-worker what they think it's worth. Yet, almost all will relate a selling price during the Description step, although wrong syntax afterward can lead to an impasse.

A wrong way:

"When you indicated you'd like to try to sell your present vehicle for seven thousand dollars," says the salesperson, "how did you arrive at that figure?"

"A co-worker offered me eight thousand dollars for it a month or so ago," replies the prospect, "but he's on vacation, and I want to get a newer vehicle before he returns. I thought I'd be nice and let you guys have it for the seven thousand dollars."

Suppose the truth is that when he'd asked everybody at his workplace to buy it one co-worker offered five thousand dollars and another offered four thousand? Unfortunately, the truth won't help him obtain a higher figure. Asking how he arrived at his selling price elicits a fabrication. The proper question is, **"Did you make any effort to try to sell your present vehicle before you came in today?"** "No" implies he hasn't tested the market...his price is a trial balloon, and he doesn't know its worth. "Yes" indicates he's attempted to sell it, but no takers. The proof is parked outside. Its value is whatever the market will bear. A selling price will continue to be reduced to market value when there are no buyers at a higher figure. Various presentations are made to the prospect after he's made a commitment to purchase a newer vehicle, while his present vehicle is being appraised by a manager. The purpose is to try to reduce in the prospect's mind what he himself believes his vehicle is worth before showing him the appraisal figure.

Five Presentations for Valuating the Trade

1. Try to Sell
2. Thorough Job
3. Genius Used Car Manager

4. Member of the Family
5. The Oscar Presentation

An important ingredient for any presentation that begins with the salesperson returning from the manager's office is the **'Progress Report'**. It prevents the prospect from becoming impatient, as he's kept abreast of the progress that's being made on his transaction by someone other than the salesperson. When progress reports are omitted, prospects look at their watches and become anxious...sometimes intimidating. The Progress Report is in bold face in each of the following presentations.

*   *   *

1. Try to Sell?

"Mr. Goodheart is working on the figures, and he'll be just a few minutes, says the salesperson. I was thinking that rather than wait for him to finish and possibly cause him to take more time, why don't I just come back here and keep you company. Is that okay?"

"That's fine," answers the prospect.

Think of the irony. The transaction will be expedited if the salesperson stays. The prospect's permission mitigates his anxiety.

"Good," says the salesperson. "By the way, when you were even considering the possibility of getting a newer vehicle,keeping in mind that you'd probably choose to try to sell your present vehicle like you're talking about, did you make any effort at all to try to find a home for your present car with any friends, neighbors, relatives, people down at work, church, anything like that?"

There are only two possibly answers.

"No," replies the prospect.

"Oh, just a minute. There may be some activity in the office relating to this. Let me see what if anything Mr. Goodheart has managed to come up with. I'll be back."

If the prospect replies with "Yes", the salesperson must leave immediately before he hears the accompanying belabored and ofttimes exaggerated story.

*   *   *

2. Thorough Job

Clean-looking vehicles occasionally hide malfunctions and serious defects, and their owners are hopeful they won't be revealed until after the sale is consummated and they're long gone. The **Thorough Job** presentation exposes them, and a litany of confessions follow as the value plummets like a stone.

"Mr. Goodheart has just left to appraise your car," says the salesperson. **"He'll be a few minutes.** By the way, do you have some gas in it?"

"Yes," responds the prospect.

"Good. I don't know how you happened to pick this particular time to come in and inquire about getting a newer vehicle, because you picked the time when Mr. Goodheart's on duty. When he appraises a vehicle, he doesn't just walk around it and kick the tires. He does a very **Thorough Job.** He'll be gone for about twenty minutes, maybe a little longer. He'll take it out on the highway, brake it real hard a few times, take it through some tight turns, even take it over to the shopping mall, drive it over a couple of speed bumps, not too fast, maybe ten-fifteen miles per hour. You see, his objective is to become as familiar with your vehicle in fifteen-twenty minutes as you are. And you've had it what now, three and a half, four, four and a half years? I do know he's been gone for a few minutes already. Let me see how much longer it'll be before he returns."

Regardless of a confession, the prospect knows well his vehicle's imperfections and that the appraiser is discovering them. Some prospects realize too late that his own gas is being used to devalue his vehicle. Conversely, an obvious 'mint condition' vehicle won't be a candidate for this presentation, because the stated value probably cannot be diminished.

*   *   *

3. Genius Used Car Manager

A disturbing aspect is the prospect's belief that the dealership makes two profits on a transaction involving a trade-in; one on the newer vehicle that is sold, the other on the prospect's trade-in when it's resold. Why shouldn't the prospect profit from his present vehicle, he wonders? This belief must be overcome before the prospect will lower his selling price. Solution: Remove the profit motive.

"Mr. Goodheart has not yet returned from looking at your car, but we expect him back very shortly," says the salesperson. "You may not already know this, but Mr. Goodheart is very highly-regarded by his peers in the automobile business, not only here in town, but throughout this entire region. He's commonly referred to as, well, a **Genius.** For two main reasons. One, because of the wonderful way he handles the needs of our customers who are interested in previously-owned vehicles; and two, because of the way he stocks them throughout the year. If you took a close look at our used vehicle inventory when you arrived today, you'd have noticed some one year olds, although not many, because people usually keep them longer than that. And you'd have noticed a good selection of two year olds and three year olds. But if you knew the exceptionally high standard that our dealer mandates for vehicles to be eligible for resale in the first place, you'd do a back flip. A vehicle must submit to a rigid, intensive, complete engine examination, all working parts, electrical and mechanical, brakes, glass, interior compartment, trunk, everything. Plus, a vehicle must get an 'A-Plus', an 'A', no less than an 'A-Minus' in every single category. If a vehicle falls short...well, in the automobile business there's a term...and you may have heard of it...wholesaling? Whether you've heard of it or not, there are people out there who are known as 'wholesalers'. They visit dealerships like ours sometimes every day, but at least once per week, and they buy the vehicles from us that didn't get the 'A's' and 'A-plusses' and pass muster. Then they spend some money on them, they fix them up a little bit, they recondition them, they repair any deficiencies and turn right around and resell them at the auction or to some used car lot; and those vehicles show up a couple of weeks later upstate or over in the next town. Let me ask you straight out, would you consider just simply keeping your present vehicle? That might help simplify things a little bit?"

"No. I don't want it," replies the prospect.

The epitome of rejection! Mission accomplished!

"Is that what you want me to tell Mr. Goodheart when he gets back from looking at it," asks the salesperson, "that you'd rather not keep it?"

"Yes," replies the prospect.

Even for wholesale, he spurns it. Ironically, while the salesperson relates the appraiser's high esteem and professional practices, the prospect visualizes his vehicle's imperfections and plummeting value. If he opts to keep it, that's a happy circumstance for the dealership.

*   *   *

4. Member of the Family.

A derogatory statement is unequivocal and always leads to plummeting value. The challenge of getting the prospect to speak derogatorily about his vehicle is solved with the use of a double entendre.

"Mr. Goodheart has just returned from looking at your car," says the salesperson. **"He's in the office right now putting the figures together. He'll be just a couple more minutes.** You know, Mr. Johnson, nobody, nobody ever has a higher regard for a vehicle than the person who already owns it. For example, think about how you feel about your present car. And why not? It's like a **Member of the Family,** isn't it? It's taken the kids to school, dad to work, the family on vacation, to the games, to the drive-in restaurants. Family togetherness. I've met folks who have such a high regard for their present cars that they even name them. You know how some people name their boats? Like the Queen Mary? Rosemary's Baby? Lady of the Lake? Usually feminine names? A while back I heard about a sweet, elderly lady, who'd come in and bought a car. But, she'd done something out of the ordinary. Instead of a feminine name, she'd named her car a man's name. Guess what that sweet lady named her car?"

"I really don't know," replies the prospect.

"Fred! She named her car Fred! Can you imagine? And the way I recall the story, the salesperson didn't know who Fred was. I guess she got a little put out about that. Turned out to be her car. By the way, you don't happen to call your car anything, do you?"

"Not really."

It's not uncommon for some prospects to look down and faintly smile. Some roll their eyes or grimace when they discern the double entendre. That assures they're thinking derogatorily about their vehicles. If the present owner has unkind thoughts about his own vehicle, why shouldn't anyone else?

"It's more common than people realize. Let me go back and see what, if anything, Mr. Goodheart has come up with."

Does the prospect's unkind thought cause the value to go up? Or down?

*   *   *

5. Oscar Presentation

The Academy Awards invented the technique of slowly opening the envelope that contains the winner's name. Everyone's dying of anticipation, particularly the nominees. Similarly, the prospect anxiously awaits the appraisal figure, although his schizophrenic expectations are seasoned with rejection and name-calling.

A perfect appraisal begins ten percent less than the prospect's selling price and ends two to three hundred dollars over the 'start figure'.

Example for an Oscar

$4550   **Start figure in Description**
Bob would like to try to sell his present vehicle for $7000, if possible.

The 'start figure' mentioned by the salesperson during the Description, in this example, was $4550. In response to that the prospect said he wanted to try to sell his present vehicle for $7000. The Description Phrase in the second box of the Description reads, "Bob would like to try to sell his present vehicle for $7000, if possible." Thus, on a handwritten appraisal, the appraiser writes the appraisal figure for $6350, which is approximately 10% less than the desired $7000 figure from the prospect. Below the $6350 he itemizes each deficiency that must be corrected, and he puts a value on it. The result Net Appraisal figure is about $200 to $300 more than the 'start figure' of $4550.

Appraisal

$6350

1.	Replace 2 front tires	170
2.	Replace front windshield.	550
3.	Minor engine tuneup.	210
4.	Repair Air-Conditioner.	90
5.	Bodywork—rear right door.	400
6.	Quartz clock broken.	65

NET APPRAISAL $4865

It is important that this be handwritten, and not a printed form. This is not the Appraisal slip that the used car manager uses when appraising vehicles. It must be easy to read, easy to understand, using language that is not 'car-talk.' The values put on these corrections need to be reasonable and competitive.

In the same way a good doctor needs a good bedside manner with his patients, the salesperson needs a good bedside manner with the prospect when he's showing the **Oscar Presentation**; and he must explain it in a clear, easy-to-understand fashion. He must refrain from using terms that 'car-people' use with each other. All jargon must be eliminated. For example, item #5 on the Oscar Presentation reads "Bodywork—rear right door.

Repaint." That is easy for the prospect to understand. But, suppose the Sales Manager wrote the words "Right quarter panel"? 'What the heck is that?' may wonder the prospect. If the prospect tried to decipher a typical Appraisal at many dealerships, he wouldn't be able to, because it is full of 'car-talk' instead of 'people-talk'.

Chapter 16

Real World

A prospect's commitment to a monthly payment is typically about sixty percent of what he's first asked. Revealing the shortage is the role of the **Real World** presentation.

In a prospect's mind, a fantasy exists regarding a vehicle's cost, as several years have elapsed since he last purchased; and his desire for a nicer model with more options, fluctuating rates, and inflation have teamed up to cause 'sticker shock'.

Giving him credit for all he's contributed to the transaction is persuasive and unchallengeable; and if the revealed shortage is several thousand dollars (or more than ten percent of the selling price), he might subsequently increase his proffered monthly payment or down payment. Or both.

How much vehicle will his committed monthly payment buy? In the following example, the prospect desires a vehicle with a sticker price of $22,100. He wants to sell his present vehicle for $6500 with a remaining payoff of $4235. He's already volunteered $1500 for a down payment on the new vehicle and made an offer in the form of a monthly payment of $450 in response to the $660 that was presented during the Commitment.

REAL WORLD DIAGRAM

(First Box)	$22,100 Regular Price
	-13,400 = How much $450/mo. will finance
	$ 8,700 Short
(Second Box)	-6,500 Prospect's present vehicle
	$ 2,200 Still short
(Second Box)	+4,235 Amount owed on present vehicle
	$ 6,435 Still short
(Third Box)	-1,500 Down payment cash
	$ 4,935 Still short

Notice how the **Real World** Diagram follows the order of the Description boxes except for **$13,400 = How much $450/mo. will finance.** Prospects love the sound of their own figures. They hate the sound of the dealership's. The first two numbers of the diagram are rounded down to double zeros...to assure being mentioned **generally** instead of **specifically**...since they're subject to challenge. A prospect won't confront his own numbers, though. That's why they can be specific. Let's listen in, commencing with the Progress Report in bold face type.

Roleplay

Salesperson:

"Duane? Julia? **Mr. Goodheart is working on everything. I'm sorry it's taking so long. He's run into a little problem, but he's trying to work it out anyway. He showed me the problem, so let me show you while he seeks a solution.**" The salesperson sets the Real World diagram atop the desk for them to see. "Remember when you mentioned that you'd like your monthly payments to be around four hundred fifty dollars per month?"

"Yes?" replies the prospect.

"Well, the way the banks work everything out, when customers want their payments to be four hundred fifty dollars per month, that's just about enough to finance thirteen thousand four hundred dollars. (See chapter entitled, Proving the Bank Figures). You may wonder how it works out that way, but it is correct, and I'll show you in a minute if you want. But in this particular case, you folks have picked out a vehicle that's much more valuable, one that's in the twenty two thousand some-odd range. Don't be concerned about that right now, because I'm making a point different from what you might think. Anyway, when you subtract thirteen thousand four hundred dollars from that, in this particular case, it shows that you're eighty seven hundred dollars short. But, you agreed to help. Remember when you said you'd sell your present vehicle for sixty five hundred? That helps, but not enough, because you're still short by twenty two hundred dollars. One thing that doesn't help is the forty two hundred thirty five dollars you still owe, so that must be added and the shortage becomes sixty four hundred thirty five dollars. You helped more, though, with the fifteen hundred dollars for the down payment? Unfortunately, that's not enough, because you're still short by forty nine hundred thirty five dollars. And that's the problem that Mr. Goodheart is grappling with. Let me see if he's managed to come up with a solution."

Someone's wrestling a giant squid. Even with the prospects' help, the shortage grows as new tentacles encircle their extremities and throats. Duane and Julia have not been asked for any of the shortage. Its enormity takes getting-used-to. Alone together, they stare at the figures. Most are theirs. They are correct. The couple might question why their payment finances only thirteen thousand four hundred dollars (See chapter entitled, Proving the Bank Figures), but their attention is fixed on the huge shortage. Solutions include 1) tooth fairy; 2) lottery; 3) huge discount; 4) more for his present vehicle; 5) huge down payment; 6) higher monthly payments. They remember being told at a different dealership that two thousand dollars would be knocked off the price. "Migawd," thinks Duane, "We're still going to be short by twenty nine hundred thirty five dollars. Mr. Goodheart can't knock forty nine hundred dollars off! We'll have to help a little…maybe with more cash for the down payment."

The **Real World**…the moment of truth…do or die, much like a soap opera with all the same absurd questions. "Will Mr. Goodheart discount the price by forty nine hundred thirty five dollars?" "Will the shortage go away?" "Will the Stuarts add a substantial sum to their down payment?" "Will Julia convince Duane to pay more per month?" "Will the salesperson have grim news when he returns?" "Has the bank made an error?" "Stay tuned."

Let's analyze.

Prospects love the sound of their own figures. They hate the sound of the dealership's. The first figure they hear is what they've already agreed to pay…four hundred fifty dollars per month.

"Mr. Goodheart has run into a little problem," says the salesperson, "but he's trying to work it out anyway. He showed me the problem, so let me show you while he seeks a solution. Remember when you mentioned that you'd like your monthly payments to be around four hundred fifty dollars per month?"

"Yes," answers the prospect.

His anxiety is eased. Mr. Nice-Guy Manager is trying to make their already committed-to payment work without asking for their help. If instead they'd heard, "You need to come up with more money," then tension would reign.

"The way the banks work everything out," continues the salesperson, "when customers want their payments to be four hundred fifty dollars per month, that's just about enough to finance thirteen thousand four hundred dollars. You may wonder how it works out that way, but that is correct, and I'll show you in a minute if you want."

No prospect will challenge the last statement if the salesperson does-n't hesitate, but all will if he asks, "Would you like me to show you right now?"

"But in this particular case," continues the salesperson, "you folks have picked out a vehicle that's much more valuable, one that's in the twenty two thousand some-odd range. Don't be concerned about that right now. I'm making a point different from what you might think."

The selling price is mentioned **generally**, "in the twenty two thousand some-odd range," which reduces the likelihood of a challenge. Bad is, "You've agreed to pay twenty two thousand one hundred dollars, right?" An important subtlety is, "picked one out" rather than "bought one for" as the syntax, because "bought" connotes the deal is final. The huge shortage mandates that all figures remain loose. The verbiage, "I'm making a point different from what you might think." is a seque **from** the selling price **to** the huge shortage.

"Anyway," says the salesperson, "when you subtract thirteen thousand four hundred dollars from that, in this particular case it shows that you're eighty seven hundred dollars short."

The pronoun, "that", substitutes for the unpleasant-sounding "selling price." A moment later, the shortage grabs their eyes and ears.

"But, you agreed to help," continues the salesperson. "Remember when you said you'd sell your present vehicle for sixty five hundred? That helps, but not enough, because you're still short by twenty two hundred dollars."

Schizophrenia rules. Duane and Julia don't know whether to be happy or sad, since their own helpful figures are quickly followed by painful shortages.

"One thing that doesn't help," adds the salesperson, "is the forty two hundred thirty five dollars you still owe, so that must be added, and the shortage becomes sixty four hundred thirty five dollars."

The salesperson needs to sound like a voodoo doctor, who's sticking pins in his Raggedy Ann lookalike.

"You helped more, though," says the salesperson, "with the fifteen hundred dollars for the down payment? Unfortunately, that's not enough, because you're still short by forty nine hundred thirty five dollars."

Hope and despair meet again. The salesperson is only the messenger…not the cause of their pain.

"And that's the problem, Mr. Goodheart is grappling with," concludes the salesperson. "Let me see if he's managed to come up with a solution."

The Real World dawns on the prospects, who will ultimately realize the necessity for more cash if they want the vehicle. They suspect that Mr. Goodheart will discover that truth, too. Little do the prospects realize that a **Double Teeter Totter** is next.

*　　　　　*　　　　　*

General Principles:

1. Use when Shortage exceeds ten percent of selling price.
2. Shortages average forty percent.
3. Manager hand-writes Real World diagram.
4. Diagram remains atop the desk when salesperson exits.
5. Prospects love the sound of their own figures.
6. Prospects hate the sound of the dealership's figures.
7. Salesperson does not ask for any of the Shortage.
8. Mention price generally, not specifically.
9. Double Teeter Totter always follows Real World.

Chapter 17

Teeter Totter and Other Playground Equipment

Teeter Totter

Most people would drive a one hundred fifty thousand dollar Rolls-Royce if the monthly payment was one hundred dollars. Most can't, though, because those figures require a one hundred forty seven thousand dollar down payment. Conversely, a zero down payment is possible with an accompanying monthly payment of three thousand seven hundred thirty two dollars. (48 months @ 9% OAC)

Such is the definition of a **Teeter Totter,** a school playground apparatus that goes up and down, and one of the greatest negotiation stratagems ever invented. When one side's down, the other's up, and vice-versa. It allows the salesperson to give the prospect whichever he wants, a low monthly payment or a low down payment, but not simultaneously.

The retail automobile business is permeated with practitioners whose ideas of negotiating are to 1) act like they're in charge of the figures

(Chairman-of-the-Board), 2) start with the most attractive-to-the-customer figures, 3) quickly slash the price against even mild opposition, and 4) maximize the finance term from the get-go. If it's true that no one likes the first figures, what can a negotiator do after he's begun with the lowest price and longest term, and the prospect rejects them? Nothing, except obtain the dealer's permission to carve up any potential profit like a Thanksgiving turkey. Ostensibly, dealers rely on their managers to make a profit, but new vehicle departments at dealerships have been money-losers since two days before water.

In 1974, in the midst of a sagging economy caused by the first-ever gas crunch, finance companies began offering forty eight month terms on car loans to make them affordable. The very next day thousands of dealerships began each negotiation at forty-eight months...taking the path of least resistance. Less than twenty five years later, seventy two month financing was prevalent. Are thirty year mortgages the future of the industry? Unfortunately, technology hasn't kept up. Planned obsolescence continues to cause maintenance and repair problems to commence at the three to four year mark. Many financed vehicles aren't candidates for resale then, because they're only half paid for. Their owners don't have enough equity for a down payment on a replacement. The payoff often exceeds the vehicle's value. Industry jargon for this affliction is "buried."

The worst thing to occur from a Teeter Totter is the prospect's unlikely rejection of the proposed increase. He'll almost always acquiesce, though, to at least a portion of it. The Real World cash shortage festers in his brain. He realizes the manager can't eliminate all of it. As he waits for the salesperson to return with the manager's response, he considers what additional down payment cash he can contribute to save the transaction. But, a surprise is in store for him.

*   *   *

Principle of Games

Simply stated, the **Principle of Games** is to do what one's opponent least expects. In boxing, the victor feints a jab and launches a left hook. The tennis player looks down the left line, then strokes a soft, cross-court lob. In football, with five seconds remaining in the fourth quarter the home team, behind by four points, has possession of the ball on its own twenty yard line; and the coach sends in Swifty Jones, the fleet-footed halfback, who trots onto the field with much fanfare and adoration. The opposing coach informs his players that "Swifty's getting the ball."

That's precisely what won't happen. The Principle of Games is at work. Swifty won't even touch the ball. His coach simply wants the opposing players to **believe** that he will, and nullify their ability to thwart the real activity...a short pass to the right end. What a simple idea, yet so uncommon in the selling game. Most prospects know what's coming next, so they're ready, their defenses are up; and confrontation occurs. What if, instead, they're not ready...hence not defensive?

Non-Confrontation occurs. The Real World presentation that precedes the Teeter Totter is like sending Swifty Jones into the game to attract attention to **what won't occur.**

            *   *   *

Example Diagram of Teeter Totter

$1500 down <> $610 month

"Duane, Julia," says the salesperson. "I may have some good news for you. Mr. Goodheart has found a way to work this out. (Headline) And for no more than the fifteen dollar down payment you already said you could come up with for the down payment. Let me tell you everything he said."

He sits down and continues without a pause. The prospects are relieved by the sound of their own figures. The additional cash they'd been prepared to offer won't be necessary, they hope. The good news keeps pouring over them.

"Mr. Goodheart said you can buy and drive this vehicle home today," says the salesperson. His presentation follows the Description Boxes, numbers one through four. "It's the one that we looked at with all the nice equipment on it that you like, the automatic transmission, cloth seats, air-conditioning, power windows, tilt wheel, the AM/FM radio with the concert hall sound and the CD player. He said he'd go ahead and buy your vehicle if you still want him to, pay it off, apply any equity to the transaction. He said he's found a way to do it so that you won't need to come up with any additional cash for the down payment over the fifteen hundred dollars that you already said was okay. And I hope you're as happy about hearing that as I am to be able to tell you. Now, in order for Mr. Goodheart to work this out and eliminate the need for any of that forty nine hundred thirty five dollar shortage that we've been concerned about, the bank is going to require that instead of your monthly payment being four hundred fifty dollars like you said you wanted, it'll be a little bit less than six hundred ten dollars. How much will that mess up your budget?"

"Six hundred ten dollars!" cries Duane. "We told you four fifty. Maybe we could do four seventy five, but not six hundred ten!"

"Four seventy five? I was afraid of that. After we spent all this time, too." The salesperson glumly turns over the Description and stares at the prospects hopelessly for ten or fifteen seconds.

Duane and Julia try not to look at each other.

"Let me ask you this, Duane and Julia," asks the salesperson finally. "I know nothing's easy, but what amount over the above the four seventy five per month could you manage, thinking about it that way?"

Duane and Julia look at each other.

"Maybe another twenty five dollars?" says Julia.

"Another twenty five dollars?" repeats the salesperson. "Duane?"

"I suppose," whispers Duane.

"What would that make it?" asks the salesperson.

"Five hundred," says Duane.

"Five hundred dollars?" repeats the salesperson.

"Yes," says Duane.

"What if it weren't so easy?" asks the salesperson. "What could you do? Darn that shortage anyway!"

This third request for an increased payment is appropriate, because each of the prospect's two increases were identical amounts, twenty five dollars. If the second increase had been less than twenty five dollars, the salesperson would need to make a judgment regarding further tension. For example, if the second increase had been five dollars (raising the payment from four seventy five to four hundred eighty), then tension is close to maximum, because the second increase is just one-fifth the size of the previous one.

"Look," says Duane. "We can go to five fifteen. But that's it."

An ultimatum accompanies the diminished increase. Arguably, it's time to slacken the rubber band.

"Nothing's ever it, Duane and Julia," says the salesperson, "but what would you like me to tell Mr. Goodheart in that regard?"

"Tell him we can pay five fifteen," replies Duane.

"Will do."

The salesperson should write the changed amount on the Description, but he must not ask Duane and Julia to sign it, as that will lock them at those figures. The prospects could threaten, "We'll okay this, but you've got to promise that nothing else will change." Negotiations would screech to a halt! The Teeter Totter presentation has raised the prospect's payment from four fifty to five fifteen per month, a sixty five dollar per month increase! If fifteen hundred down caused the payment to be $610, what will the down payment need to be for a five hundred fifteen dollar monthly payment? For the first time in the manager's calculation, he considers forty eight months, causing the Teeter Totter to become:

Diagram of Teeter Totter

Was	Now
$1500 down <> $610 month	**$2700 down <> $515 month**

And, the salesperson's presentation begins with, "Mr. Goodheart has found a way to work this out for the five fifteen payment...", is followed by the **Good News,** and ends with the bank's requirement of twenty seven hundred dollars instead of fifteen hundred for the down payment. If the prospects respond with an increased down payment, then another Teeter Totter is appropriate that contains a request for an increased monthly payment.

Diagram of Teeter Totter

$2000 down <> $540 month

Teeter Totters maximize a salesperson's ability to elicit more down payment monies and higher monthly payments without confrontation, which provide for stronger contracts, better lender relationships, shorter terms, faster payoff, more frequent trade-in cycles, better-condition trade-ins, and equity buildup concurrent with vehicle buyers' expectations. These benefits are lost when the first proffer to a prospect is seventy two month financing. If the reader accepts the premise that the prospect never likes the first figures, what's the plan to maintain profit and obtain viable down payment cash **after** the lowest figures and longest term are presented first?

*   *   *

Double Teeter Totter

The small difference between a Teeter Totter and a **Double Teeter Totter** creates stunning improvements in the amounts that are generated. Here's the difference: A Teeter Totter adds zero to one side and a large amount to the other each time; whereas a Double Teeter Totter adds a token amount to one side and a large amount to the other.

Diagram of Teeter Totter   **Diagram of Double Teeter Totter**

$1500 down <> $610 month   2850 down <> $450+40=$490)

After the Real World, the prospects realize that the manager can't eliminate the entire huge shortage, and opts to help save the transaction by contributing more down payment cash. The salesperson's helpful attitude allow them to blurt out agreement for the token addition, but Godzilla's foot still shows up at the end in spite of the seemingly temporary relief.

"Duane and Julia," says the salesperson, "I'm sorry this is taking so long, but Mr. Goodheart has managed to find a way to work this out...but the way he's found will not enable him to get your monthly payment **all the way down to** the four hundred fifty dollars that you said you wanted. You are going to have to raise your sights a little bit on your monthly payment. And when I say a little bit, it may sound like a little, it may sound like a lot; but however it sounds, it'll be right around forty five dollars in addition to the four hundred fifty you already said you could do. And before you say anything, quite frankly if you can't see fit to do that, it's pointless for me to go ahead and show you what Mr. Goodheart has worked out."

"I guess we can do that," replies Duane.

The salesperson looks at Julia. "That would be all right?" he asks.

"Yes," she answers.

The prospects' acquiescence is common, because the increased payment sounds so trivial compared to the huge shortage they've been worried about; and even if they don't accept all of the payment's increase, they'll almost-always accept a large portion. It's as easy as it sounds, and veteran salespeople wonder why they haven't known about this years ago.

The prospects realize they won't hear the manager's solution until they agree, which is part of their compulsion to do so. If they don't, however, the salesperson must return to the manager without relating it.

"Then let me tell you all the details," continues the salesperson. Mr. Goodheart said you can buy and drive this vehicle home today. It's the one that we looked at with all the nice equipment on it that you like, the automatic transmission, cloth seats, air-conditioning, power windows, tilt wheel, the AM/FM radio with the concert hall sound and the CD player. He said he'd go ahead and buy your vehicle if you still want him to, pay it off, apply any equity to the transaction. And the way he's found to do it is for your monthly payment to be about forty five dollars over and above the four hundred fifty dollars you'd already said you could manage, which will make somewhere around four hundred ninety five or so. And I hope you're as pleased about hearing that as I am to tell you? Are you?"

"That sounds okay," replies Duane.

Here comes **Godzilla's Foot** without any warning!

"Fine," says the salesperson. "Now, Duane and Julia, in order for Mr. Goodheart to be able to work this all out, the bank, the bank, you know, the bank is going to require that instead of the fifteen hundred dollars you said you could come up with for the down payment, they're going to require a little bit less than twenty eight hundred fifty dollars altogether. How much will that mess up your budget?"

Godzilla has ridden the elevator up from the fourth box to the third, changing the discussion from monthly payment amount to down payment cash. The prospects have already accepted a forty to forty five dollar monthly payment increase.

"Twenty eight fifty!" cries Duane. "We told you fifteen hundred. Maybe we could do another five hundred, but not that much."

"Another five hundred?" repeats the salesperson with a disappointed tone.

"Yes," replies Duane.

"What would that make it?" asks the salesperson.

"Two thousand," replies Duane.

"Mmm," murmurs the salesperson. He glumly turns over the Description. "Let me ask you this, Duane and Julia," continues the salesperson after a couple of beats. "I know nothing's easy, but what amount over and above the two thousand could you manage, thinking about it that way?"

Duane and Julia look at each other.

"That's more than we'd planned on," responds Julia.

"That's how it sounds," says the salesperson.

"See if the two thousand will work," offers Duane.

"Is that what you want me to tell Mr. Goodheart?" asks the salesperson.

"Yes," replies Duane.

The **Double Teeter Totter** should always follow a Real World, and a Teeter Totter should almost always follow a Double Teeter Totter. The salesperson's characterization of the dialogue will greatly assist the manager to structure the Teeter Totter that follows, as he'll add to the side of the Teeter Totter that's most pliable. Duane and Julia accepted the forty-five dollar payment increase easily, and the five hundred dollar down payment increase reluctantly. Subsequently, the next Teeter Totter will leave the two thousand dollar down payment alone and add fifteen dollars to the monthly payment.

Diagram of Teeter Totter

$2000 down <> $495+15 = $510 month

Theoretically, Teeter Tottering back and forth can continue until the prospects no longer elevate their figures, although a typical transaction contains one Double Teeter Totter and two Teeter Totters. A good tactic is to add a Teeter Totter when the salesperson and manager believe that Duane and Julia will tolerate no more, because the prospects will reject that final increase in entirety and claim a victory of negotiation. A good deal is a state-of-mind.

*   *   *

Analyzing the Verbiage

"Duane and Julia," says the salesperson, "I'm sorry this is taking so long, but Mr. Goodheart has managed to find a way to work this out…but the way he's found will not enable him to get your monthly payment all the way down to the four hundred fifty dollars that you said you wanted."

The wording, "all the way down to" implies "almost" all the way down, but not quite. The prospects have been greatly concerned about the shortage, so this change of subject is a refreshing delight. Their desired mental response is, "We'll do anything about the monthly payment if we don't need to worry about that dreadful shortage."

*   *   *

"You are going to have to raise your sights a little bit on your monthly payment," says the salesperson. "And when I say a little bit, **it may sound like a little…it may sound like a lot…**"

Avoidance of argument is the goal of this text. Omit the boldfaced phrase, and the prospect's angry retort after hearing the amount could be, "That's not a little bit!"

*   *   *

"…but however it sounds," continues the salesperson, "it'll be right around forty five dollars in addition to the four hundred fifty you already said you could do."

Never add more than ten percent to the payment with a Double Teeter Totter, because the high acceptance rate will plummet. Greed costs. Keep in mind that the remaining deficiency will be included in the down payment increase. "Token" characterizes the payment increase. Over ten percent is not that.

*   *   *

"And before you say anything, quite frankly if you can't see fit to do that, it's pointless for me to go ahead and show you what Mr. Goodheart has worked out."

The prospects' desire to see Mr. Goodheart's solution will only be satisfied with their verbal acceptance of the token payment increase. Anything short of that keeps it undisclosed. For example, if the prospects responded, "We can pay twenty five more, but not forty five," then the salesperson would need to return to the manager, because nonacceptance of the total "token" will change the remaining figure in the Double Teeter Totter. The salesperson's exit statement would be, "That's going to change everything. Let me inform Mr. Goodheart and see how that's going to effect what he's worked out for you."

*   *   *

"I guess we can do that," says Duane.

"That would be all right?" asks the salesperson of Julia.

"Yes," agrees Julia.

Guess is a Weasel word, and it must be eliminated before proceeding.

*   *   *

"Then let me tell you all the details," says the salesperson. "Mr. Goodheart said you can buy and drive this vehicle home today..."

The salesperson proceeds through the Description boxes commencing with number one to the down payment increase and determines what amount, if any, the prospects will accept.

Example: $15,000 Regular Price

-0-	Desired Down
350	Monthly payment commitment

To finance $15,000 with zero down payment for 36 months @ 9% interest, the required monthly payment is $477. The prospect's commitment is $350, a $127 shortage. The down payment that's needed to buy the monthly payment down to $350 is $3994.

Chapter 18

Proving the Bank Figures

The Real World presentation in chapter sixteen informed the prospects that their committed payment of four hundred fifty dollars per month financed thirteen thousand four hundred dollars. For a fast calculation, the manager used a factor (.0336), which he divided into the monthly payment ($450) to determine what amount ($13,400) the payment would finance. The factor (.0336) is based on twelve percent APR with a thirty six month term.

$450 divided by .0336 = $13,392.85 rounded to $13,400. The factor changes with the prevailing interest rate.

Factor Conversion Chart

6% APR = .0310 14% APR = .0344
8% APR = .0319 16% APR = .0352
10% APR = .0328 18% APR = .0361
12% APR = .0336 20% APR = .0369

Since the late 1970's, interest rates have ranged from a high of twenty two percent APR to a low of zero during special promotions. The median rate of twelve percent APR interest is used throughout this book.

Here's a response to a prospect's query.

"How does the bank arrive at that?" asks Duane.

"Let me show you," answers the salesperson. "Let's say you borrowed thirteen thousand four hundred dollars from the bank. Do you know the current interest rate at your bank?"

"Around twelve percent?" replies Duane.

His most probable answer is the current rate. Whatever rate he mentions, though, must be used to satisfy his query. Two percentage points alter the payment about eleven dollars for this balance.

"It's your bank," says the salesperson. "Let's use that for our example. Twelve percent interest is APR, the Annualized Percentage Rate. You're familiar with that, aren't you?"

"Yes," replies Duane.

"To quickly calculate the total interest payable over the term of a contract, the bank first converts the APR interest into what they refer to as add-on interest. Twelve percent APR is about the same as seven percent add-on. (See Conversion Table below) The bank multiplies the add-on interest times the number of years in the contract. For example, three years times seven percent add-on equals twenty one percent. Four years times seven percent add-on equals twenty eight percent. Even though I'm exaggerating slightly to make my point, I want to keep the interest amount down, so I'm showing you twenty one percent for three years instead of twenty eight percent for four. The bank multiplies thirteen thousand four hundred, the amount that four hundred fifty dollars per month will finance, times twenty one percent, and the answer becomes two thousand eight hundred fourteen dollars, the total interest charged by the bank over three years. It's one-third that amount for one year. Even more than that for four years. See how it works? The bank adds the interest to the principal, and the total becomes sixteen thousand two hundred fourteen dollars. The bank divides that figure by the number of months in the contract, and the monthly payment becomes four hundred fifty dollars thirty eight cents. Mr. Goodheart's payment was off by only thirty eight cents! But in this particular case, you folks have picked out a vehicle that is much more valuable..."

The Salesperson continues toward the huge shortage.

*   *   *

Diagram of Proof

$13,400	12% = 7% Add-On x 3 years = 21%
x 21%	
$ 2814	Interest
+13,400	Principal
$16,214	divided by 36 = $450.38 per month

Reread the dialogue while looking at the diagram.

Virtually no prospect will ask to increase the term because the total interest will increase incrementally. He heard the salesperson say, "...to keep the interest amount down, I'm showing you twenty one percent for three years instead of twenty eight percent for four." A salesperson can derail the process by inviting unnecessary queries. Examples include: "Would you like to see how much less the payment will be for four-five-six years?" and "Should I use the three year example or the four year example?"

*   *   *

Converting APR into Add-On Interest Chart

General principle: Divide APR by 2 and add 1.

6% APR = 4% Add-on	6 divided by 2 + 1 = 4
8% APR = 5% Add-on	8 divided by 2 + 1 = 5
10% APR = 6% Add-on	10 divided by 2 + 1 = 6
12% APR = 7% Add-on	12 divided by 2 + 1 = 7
14% APR = 8% Add-on	14 divided by 2 + 1 = 8
16% APR = 9% Add-on	16 divided by 2 + 1 = 9
18% APR = 10% Add-on	18 divided by 2 + 1 = 10
20% APR = 11% Add-on	20 divided by 2 + 1 = 11

Fractions and odd-number APR rates should be converted as follows for approximations.

1. **Round up the APR rate to an even number.**
2. **Divide the even number by 2.**
3. **Add 1.**

Example:
APR is 9%.
Round 9 up to an even number...10.
Divide 10 by 2 = 5.
Add 1 to 5 = 6% Add-on = 9% APR

Another example:
APR is 7.5%
Round 7.5 up to an even number...8.
Divide 8 by 2 = 4
Add 1 to 4 = 5% Add-on = 7.5% APR

Although the conversion is not exact, its within half a point in most cases. The wording, "even though I'm exaggerating a little bit" is important for that reason. Whole numbers are simpler to relate and understand; whereas, "13% APR equals 7.47231%" sounds pompous and confusing.

Oddly, 2.9% APR does not allow the conversion method to work. Round 2.9% up to an even number = 4. Divide by 2 = 2. Add 1 = 3. Hence, the add-on is higher than the APR. Solution: Convert 2.9% APR to 2% Add-on, and it'll be close.

Chapter 19

The Telephone

Approximately half of the prospects who visit an automobile dealership phone first. Even if only one tenth did, telephone skills are obligatory.

Why do prospects phone first rather than make a personal appearance? So they can be anonymous, **get** information, and vanish. The telephone company coined an appropriate slogan, "Let your fingers do the walking." The caller strives to get information and give none. Ironically, shortly after the caller receives the information he hangs up. Here's a typical situation.

Unskilled salesperson answers the phone.

"Sales," says the salesperson.

"Hello," says the caller. "I saw your ad for the 4-wheel drive pickup? Do you still have it?"

"Sure do," answers the salesperson. "I'm looking right at it."

"Thanks," says the caller.

The line goes dead. What if the caller does show up? Does he know the salesperson's name? And vice versa?

Another typical bad situation.

"Sales department," says the salesperson.

"I'm looking at your ad for the new convertible for twenty one thousand seven hundred ninety nine," volunteers the caller. "Is that your best price?"

"Are you kidding?" asks the salesperson. "I'm sure we can work out just about anything you want when you come in and take a look at it."

"Thanks," says the caller. "Maybe I'll drop by after work."

The line goes dead. This situation is worse than the first, because the caller has a reasonable expectation that the advertised price will be substantially reduced. If he appears, and it isn't, guess what?

Let's define two terms, **Inanimate Objects** and **Communications.**

*   *   *

Inanimate Objects

Three dictionary definitions:
1. Not having the qualities associated with active, living organisms.
2. Not animate.
3. Grammar. Belonging to the class of nouns that stand for nonliving things.

In both situations the salesperson was an **inanimate object.** His first greetings were "Sales" and "Sales department." When one meets an individual in person, does he say, "Sales."

Idiotic, isn't it? If so, why not by phone? Inanimate objects don't match up with prospects any more than a fencepost would, or a door, or lead weight.

*   *   *

Communications, a Definition

Two dictionary definitions:
1. The act of communicating, transmission.

2.   a). The exchange of thoughts, messages, or information, as by speech, signals, writing, or behavior.

b). Interpersonal rapport.

c). The art or technique of using words effectively and with grace in imparting one's ideas.

In either situation was there any exchange of thoughts? What about interpersonal rapport? Or "grace of imparting..."? The salesperson could just as well have been the elevator voice.

The best definition:

Communications occurs from the receiver to the sender, not from the sender to the receiver. This definition is paramount. Carve it upon one's desk, graffiti on the overpass, marble letters atop the Acropolis. Once the reader accepts this premise and definition, his communication skills soar.

A wrong way.

"What's your telephone number?" asks the salesperson.

"555-2628," replies the caller.

"Thanks," asks the salesperson.

What's wrong with it? Everything! Communications occurs **from** the receiver **to** the sender, not from the sender to the receiver. In the foregoing, did the receiver of the information return it to the sender? No, he only received it.

The proper way.

"What's your telephone number?" asks the salesperson.

"555-2628," replies the caller.

"Your number is 555-2628?" clarifies the salesperson.

"That's correct," replies the caller.

The salesperson simply repeats the information he's received from the caller, and good communications occur.

Another wrong way:

"Jerry," says the boss, "I'm calling a special sales meeting for Thursday morning at 8 a.m. Be sure you notify everybody."

"Will do," says Jerry.

The following Thursday, no one shows up. The boss confronts Jerry, who explains, "I thought you meant **next** Thursday." The missing ingredient? The communications didn't go from the receiver to the sender.

The right way:

"Jerry," says the boss, "I'm calling a special sales meeting for Thursday morning at 8 a.m. Be sure you notify everybody."

"The meeting's this Thursday at 8 a.m.," repeats Jerry, "and, you want me to notify the sales staff and all managers?"

"That's correct," replies the boss.

"Will do," says Jerry.

The boss knows that Jerry knows, and Jerry knows that the boss knows that he knows. The meeting's less likely to go awry, and more likely to be successful. Jerry (the receiver) repeated the information back to the boss (the sender), and good communications occurred.

Another wrong way: Hotel guest phones front desk to request a wake-up call.

"Front desk," says the innkeeper.

"I'm Mr. Wayfarer in room 1416," says the caller. "Will you give me a wake-up call at 6:30?"

"Will do," replies the innkeeper. "Good night."

Will the innkeeper answer other calls before he completes this task? Will he record it accurately regardless of whether he has interruptions? Is he error-proof? Does Mr. Wayfarer know that the innkeeper knows? Will he toss and turn?

The right way:

"I certainly will, Mr. Wayfarer," replies the innkeeper. "You wish a wakeup call tomorrow morning at six thirty. Room 1416. I'm putting it in my computer as we speak. Good night, Mr. Wayfarer."

"Good night."

Good communications require very little effort or time...only discipline. Now the guest can sleep like a baby.

Recap:

1. Don't be an inanimate object.
2. Communications occur from the receiver to the sender…not from the sender to the receiver.

In the following dialogue, the salesperson practices good communications principles, puts the caller at ease, opts not to be an inanimate object, obtains and provides good information, improves the likelihood that the caller will visit the dealership and seek him out.

       *   *   *

Good Phone Conversation

The salesperson picks up the phone after hearing a page that there's a call for the Sales Department.

"Hello. My name is Jimmy. Jimmy Dover. What is your name?"

"My name is Gary Shultsman."

"Shultsman. Is your last name spelled S-C-H-U-L-T-Z-M-A-N?"

"No. It's S-H-U-L-T-S-M-A-N."

"Oh. S-H-U-L-T-S-M-A-N. With an S. Sorry I misspelled it. My last name is spelled D-O-V-E-R. Dover. Jimmy Dover. Are you calling about our ad?"

"Well, yes. I see where you've got a few late-model pickups, and I wanted to see if you have any one or two year old ones with 4-wheel drive and club cab?"

"Are you calling about a vehicle like that because it's similar to the one you're presently driving?"

"No. I drive a Mustang, but I've been looking to replace it with a pickup."

"You drive a Mustang? What year is it?"

"It's a YEAR. (three years old)"

"The reason I'm sounding so exclamatory, Mr. Shultsman, is because just recently Mr. Goodfellow, our used car manager, was looking for a vehicle kind of like that for another customer. (This is a **carrot**). You mean you might be thinking of selling it?"

"Well sure, if the price is right."

"Mr. Goodfellow will be very pleased to hear that. By the way, Mr. Shultsman, you cannot imagine the tremendous activity that our ad has caused at the dealership. (This is a **carrot**). In fact, it's so noisy you can probably hear the commotion over the phone. Will you speak up a little bit?"

"Can you hear me better?" exclaimed Mr. Shultsman in a louder voice.

"Yes. Thank you. By the way, in case we get cut off by one of the other telephone lines, may I get your number so I can call you right back?" (This is a **carrot**).

"Okay. My number is 555-8724."

"Let me write that down. 555-8274?"

"No. It's 555-8724."

"Oh. 555-8724?"

"Yes."

"Fine. By the way, Mr. Shultsman, are you calling from home?"

"Yes, I am."

"Well, let me ask you this, Mr. Shultsman, **if you get a newer vehicle, will that make you a 2-vehicle family?**"

"No. I'm single. One's enough."

"Well, let me ask you this, Mr. Shultsman, on your Mustang **is there any equipment you particularly like that you would like to have again if you replace it with a pickup? For example, do you have a preference for a stick shift or an automatic?**"

"Automatic."

"How important is air-conditioning?"

"Very important."

"What about the radio?"

"A CD would be nice this time."

"If you get a newer truck, how important would it be to be able to store things behind the driver's seat."

"Not very."

"Would anyone besides you drive it?"

"No."

"What would be an example of the heaviest load you'd have?"

"My two motorcycles."

"Would you be towing anything with it?"

"I've got a 14 foot aluminum boat on a trailer."

"Do you use your Mustang now for that?"

"Yes, I have a trailer hitch."

"By the way, the dealer here, Mr. Walters, is so pleased about the tremendous response we've been getting that he's talking about repeating this same promotion next year too!" (This is a **carrot**).

"That's nice."

The salesperson knows that four carrots provide excellent odds for success in obtaining an appointment. So he begins that development.

"Well, let me ask you this, Mr. Shultsman, are you looking for information about a truck because you're desirous of getting a newer vehicle right away, or are you simply making an inquiry for several months from now?"

"Oh, I'm looking to get a truck right away when I find what I'm looking for."

"You mean that if we have what you might be looking for, you'd come down today or later on this afternoon?"

"That's why I'm calling."

"Well, great! By the way, when you say today sometime, would you be thinking later on this afternoon?"

"That would be best for me?"

The salesperson knows the Match Up is complete, so it's relationship-building time.

"If you could give me an approximate time, I can see if that works good for me, too. By the way, Mr. Shultsman, would you prefer I continue referring to you by your last name?"

"Gary's fine."

"Well, thank you...Gary. Please call me Jimmy. You mean around three or four o'clock? Something like that?"

"Four will work."

"Let me check my schedule to see if that's good for me. Let me put the phone down for a moment. Is that okay?"

"Yes."

Jimmy sets the phone down and walks across the room to his planning calendar on the wall. He needs to convey to all prospects that he's **always** busy and has an appointment calendar, just like any professional such as a doctor or dentist or accountant. Many car-buyers believe the opposite, that salesperson sit around all day and drink coffee.

He returns to the phone. "Mr. Shultsman, I mean Gary?" he says.

"Yes?" replies Gary.

"I just checked my schedule. Four o'clock or shortly after will be perfect for me. Is that still good for you?"

"That'll work."

"Fine. Have you ever been to Walters Motors before?"

"You're on East Broadway, aren't you?"

"That's right. What direction would you be coming from at that time?"

"I'm out here at Melody Heights."

"Well, just pull into our huge driveway from Broadway and park right in front of our new vehicle showroom. When you enter the glass doors, you'll see the receptionist, Maxine, at the big white desk. Tell Maxine that you've got an appointment with me, Jimmy Dover. She'll ring my office, and I'll be right there.

Do you feel okay with those directions, Gary?"

"Yes."

"Good. I'm going to ask you one favor. You don't have to, but let me put in my request. If something should come up for you anytime between now and two o'clock that would cause you to know for certain you can't make it at four o'clock, would you please call me so I can make arrangements to see someone else at that time? And, I'll do the same for you."

"Sure. But I'll be there."

"I'm looking forward to meeting you in person."

After hanging up, the salesperson should immediately notify the Receptionist and inform her about the scheduled appointment. When the prospect arrives, the Receptionist will be expecting him.

"Hello. I've come to see Mr. Dover," says Gary to Maxine.

"Mr. Shultsman?" she says without hesitation.

"Yes."

"Mr. Dover is expecting you. Let me ring his office."

Who wouldn't like to be treated like this?

              *   *   *

Let's reverse the situation. The receptionist is unaware of the appointment. A wrong way:

"Hello. I've come to see Mr. Dover," says Gary to Maxine.

"Is he expecting you?" she asks.

"Yes."

"What's your name,?"

"Gary Shultsman. I talked to him just before noon."

Maxine turns to a salesperson, who is sitting near the window. "Fred, have you seen Jimmy?" she asks.

"He may have gone to lunch." replies Fred.

Is there any prospect who'd be impressed? Is Mr. Shultsman being made to feel important? Is professionalism anywhere? But, who's responsible for the receptionist knowing? Or not knowing?

              *   *   *

Returning to the proper way, another ingredient for good appointment preparation occurs ten minutes before the appointed time. During situations when the prospect has inquired about a specific vehicle, the salesperson should arrange to park that vehicle in a highly-visible location, and attach a hand-written note to the steering wheel that reads, "Reserved for Gary Shultsman." Special people deserve special treatment. And, if a potential customer isn't special, then who is?

*   *   *

Moral Obligation

Asking the prospect to notify the salesperson within a reasonable period of time before the actual appointment if he can't make it…and his promise to do so…is the **Moral Obligation.** When the phone call includes the Moral Obligation, the odds that the prospect will appear soar; but when not included, plummet.

One reason why some appointment prospects are 'No-Shows' is they don't perceive the cost to the salesperson. The 'No-Show' believes the salesperson can simply talk to another prospect during the time period he'd booked. Reality is that the appointment causes the salesperson to preclude all other activities for about thirty minutes before to one or two hours afterward. It's problematic for the salesperson to commence another activity shortly before an appointment, because the appointment's timely appearance will interfere…and both will be compromised. Moreover, a 'No-Show' prevents a salesperson to immediately pursue other activities. Optimistic and hopeful, the salesperson waits like an expectant father for a reasonable time and cedes other opportunities. A No-Show typically costs the salesperson at least two hours of productivity. Since the 'No-Show' places no value on a salesperson's time, the onus is on the salesperson to value his own time,—hence the Moral Obligation.

In the preceding dialogue, the salesperson placed value on his time by informing the caller that scheduled appointments are common practice as evidenced by his appointment book. If he'd said, "Anytime is good. I'm here until eight o'clock tonight," his time would have appeared worthless, as he's conveyed a blank slate.

"I'm going to ask you one favor." asks the salesperson. "You don't have to, but let me put in my request. If something should come up for you anytime between now and two o'clock that would cause you to know for certain you can't make it at four o'clock, would you please call me so I can make arrangements to see someone else at that time? And, I'll do the same for you."

"Sure. But I'll be there."

'Within a reasonable period of time' is subjective. When the appointment is the following morning, the dialogue can alter to:

"If something should come up for you anytime between now and this evening around dinnertime that would cause you to know for certain you can't make it…"

And if the appointment is imminent…two hours off…then:

"…If something should come up for you within the next hour that would cause you to know for certain you can't make it…"

Or if the appointment is a week from next Tuesday, then:

"…If something should come up for you anytime between now and the Friday before our appointment that would cause you to know for certain you can't make it…"

Moral Obligation must be an element of each appointment call, regardless of when, to improve the number of callers that show up as promised.

*　　　*　　　*

Mental Trip

The caller doesn't know what the salesperson looks like, so upon arrival anyone he sees could be Jimmy Dover. Not everyone on the sales staff makes a good first impression. Some are smokers, a few oblivious, others huddled with co-workers relating off-color stories. Is one the telephone voice? Shudder. The **Mental Trip** contained in the phone conversation described Maxine seated at her "big white desk" and Mr. Dover in his office. As a result, all others are invisible.

"Just pull into our huge driveway," says the salesperson, "from Broadway and park right in front of our new vehicle showroom. When you enter the glass doors, you'll see the receptionist, Maxine, at the big white desk. Tell Maxine that you've got an appointment with Jimmy Dover. She'll ring my office, and I'll be right there."

For many, visiting an automobile dealership is scary, and the slightest aberration repels them. The Mental Trip prepares the caller for the best possible first impression. He visualizes driving onto the dealership lot, parking in front, walking through the glass doors to Maxine's big white desk, and watching her ring Mr. Dover's office. No gauntlet of salespeople, only a yellow brick road covered with scented herbs and the highly-visible desired vehicle waiting with his name on the steering wheel.

*   *   *

Carrots

A **Carrot,** by definition, is a compelling reason for the caller to visit the dealership. Here's a Carrot list.

1. Special Event
2. Special Purchase
3. Factory Rebate
4. Lower Interest Rates
5. Special Selection
6. Lease Returns
7. Year-End Clearance
8. Crowded showroom
9. Too much inventory
10. Desired vehicle is available
11. Seeking good trade-ins
12. Looking for a vehicle similar to caller's
13. Response exceeds expectations

14. Busy phone lines may get cut off
15. Several others to choose from
16. Special Program will help reduce payments
17. Special Program will reduce down payment
18. Size of dealership
19. Repeating promotion by acclamation
20. And on and on.

General Rule: **Always give the caller four carrots before requesting an appointment.** If the salesperson offers only one carrot, the caller probably won't come in. Even if he does, he usually won't remember the salesperson's name. This is one of the more difficult telephone disciplines to maintain, because the salesperson gets excited when the caller sounds cooperative.

*　　　　　　*　　　　　　*

A Phone Conversation Gets Derailed

"Hello, my name is Barry Rogers," says the salesperson as he picks up the phone. "What is your name?"

"My name is Rose Matthews," replies the caller.

"Thanks for calling, Rose Mathews. Is your last name spelled M-A-T-H-E-W-S?"

"No. It has two T's."

"Oh. M-A-T-T-H-E-W-S. Sorry I misspelled it. My last name is spelled R-O-G-E-R-S. Rogers. Are you calling about our ad?"

"No. Late last night I drove by and noticed that two year old Dodge minivan, the green one? If you still have it, I want to stop by after work in a couple of hours to look at it."

"It's sitting right out front, Ms Matthews. Be sure to ask for Barry."

"Okay. Goodbye."

What's wrong? The caller offered her name without opposition. She volunteered to appear. Good start, but consider that she may be calling other dealerships. The only information the salesperson obtained was her name and that she's employed. When Rose got the information she sought, she hung up. He resides in Spokane, Washington. Reread the dialogue and confirm it contains just one Carrot...Desired vehicle is available. Three Carrots to go, and in Rose's case, they would have been easily obtained.

*   *   *

A Good Phone Conversation (following the introduction)

"Are you calling about our ad?" asks Jimmy Dover.

"No," replies Rose. "Late last night I drove by and noticed that two year old Dodge minivan...the green one? If you still have it, I want to stop by after work in a couple of hours to look at it."

"Is one of the reasons you're interested in looking at the minivan," asks Jimmy, **"because it's similar to the vehicle you're presently driving?"**

"No. I drive a Buick Century, but it's not big enough now for our three kids."

"Do any of them drive?"

"Omigosh, no. My oldest is only seven years old."

"How old is your Buick Century?"

"It's a MAKE/MODEL." (four years old)

"The reason I'm sounding so exclamatory, Ms Matthews, is because just recently Mr. Goodfellow, our used car manager, was looking for a vehicle kind of like that for another customer. (This is a **carrot**). You mean you might be thinking of selling it?"

"That's our plan."

"Mr. Goodfellow will be very pleased to hear that. By the way, Ms Matthews, you cannot imagine the tremendous activity that our ad has caused at the dealership. (This is a **carrot**). In fact, it's so noisy you can probably hear the commotion over the phone. Will you speak up a little bit?"

"Can you hear me better?" she exclaimed in a louder voice."

"Yes. Thank you. By the way, in case we get cut off by one of the other telephone lines, may I get your number so I can call you right back?" (This is a **carrot**).

"My number is 555-8724."

"Let me write that down. 555-8274?"

"No. It's 555-8724."

"Oh. 555-8724?"

"Yes."

"Fine. By the way, Ms Matthews, are you calling from work?"

"Yes, but please call me Rose."

"Well, let me ask you this, Rose, **if you get a newer vehicle, will that make you a 2-vehicle family?**"

"Yes. My husband drives his Ford pickup."

"A Ford pickup? Wow. What year is it?"

"It's a MAKE/MODEL." (two years old)

"Well, let me ask you this, Rose, on your Buick **is there any equipment you particularly like that you'd like to have again if you replace it with a minivan? For example, do you have a preference for a stick shift or an automatic?**"

"Automatic."

"How important is air-conditioning?"

"Very important."

"What about the radio?"

"A CD would be nice."

Rose has not yet learned whether the green minivan is still available, but the salesperson has obtained much information about her and her wants, as he's asked her three FBI Interrogation School Questions already.

"I feel so lucky, Rose," replies the Jimmy, " because based on what you've told me, there's more than one minivan that fits your description that you can take a look at. (This is a **carrot**). How soon after you get off work can you be here?"

The salesperson has been counting the carrots, and he's up to four. The time is ripe to ask for an appointment.

"I'm only fifteen minutes away," replies Rose. "I get off work at five thirty."

"Are you saying sometime between five forty-five and six-o'clock?"

"Yes."

"Let me check my schedule to see if that's good for me. Let me put the phone down for a moment. Is that okay?"

"Yes."

Jimmy sets the phone down and walks across the room to his planning calendar on the wall, then returns to the phone.

"Rose?" he says.

"Yes?"

"I just checked my schedule. Just before six o'clock or shortly thereafter is a good time. Is that still good for you?"

"Perfect."

"What direction will you be coming from?"

"My office is downtown in the Hastings Building."

*   *   *

Mental Trip

"Well, just pull into our huge driveway from Broadway and park right in front of our new vehicle showroom. When you enter the glass doors, you'll see the receptionist, Maxine, at the big white desk. Tell Maxine that you've got an appointment with me, Jimmy Dover. She'll ring my office, and I'll be right there.

Do you feel okay with those directions, Rose?"

"Yes."

*   *   *

Moral Obligation

"Good," says Jimmy. "I'm going to ask you one favor. You don't have to, but let me put in my request. If something should come up for you anytime between now and four o'clock that would cause you to know for certain you can't make it at around six, would you please call me so I can make arrangements to see someone else at that time? And, I'll do the same for you."

"Sure. But I'll be there."

"I'm looking forward to meeting you in person. Carve my name in your desk."

"I already have. It's Jimmy Dover."

By not omitting any principles or taking shortcuts (even when an appointment seemed assured) the salesperson reduced the chances this caller would phone any other dealerships before the appointed time, obtained more information about the caller and a better description of the desired vehicle, held out for at least four carrots before requesting an appointment, and included the **Mental Trip** and the **Moral Obligation.**

Chapter 20

The Twelve Commandments

1. Prospects buy from individuals they like.
2. Prospects never like the first price.
3. Prospects must never talk to the Chairman-of-the-Board before the result.
4. Never represent yourself.
5. The main purpose for each selling step is to get to the next one.
6. Like outside…buy inside.
7. Ask about the known to discover the unknown.
8. Prospects reach out for what they believe they cannot attain.
9. Practice the Principle of Games…doing what the prospect least expects.
10. Prospects love the sound of their own figures and spurn the seller's figures.
11. Non-buyers must leave with their own figures…never the seller's.
12. No competitor can ever beat the prospect's figures and earn a profit.

About the Author

John R. Downes preached NonConfrontation Selling throughout the United States, Canada, and Australia since 1979. The National Automobile Dealers Association refers to him as "the Billy Graham of sales training." His books include *How to Be Irresistible Through the Power of Persuasion* and the mystery novel, *A Few Deadly Friends.*